HAWAII
Gem of the Pacific

HAWAII

GEM OF THE PACIFIC

———————— ★ ————————

by OSCAR LEWIS

Illustrated by STEPHEN MEDVEY

Landmark BOOKS

RANDOM HOUSE · NEW YORK

Contents

HAWAII

Gem of the Pacific

1

The Setting

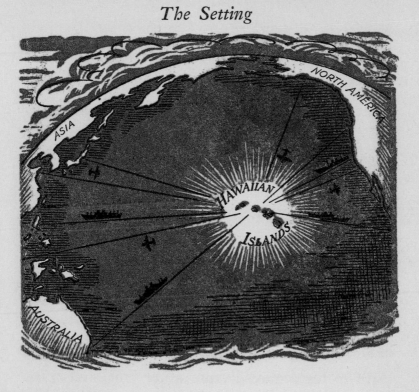

THE HAWAIIAN ISLANDS HAVE BEEN A PART OF the United States for well over half a century. The inhabitants live under the American flag, attend American schools, and play American games. In general they live much the same lives as those in other parts of the country.

Yet, the island people are unlike their fellow Americans in many ways. For one thing they are separated by great distances from the rest of the nation. More than 2,000 miles of ocean lie between their homes and the mainland. They inhabit a group of islands rising above the surface of the Pacific Ocean, the largest body of water in the world.

The people of these islands have no near neighbors. The other inhabited islands of the Pacific lie to the south and west, and all are many hundreds of miles distant. The California coast, which is the nearest point on the mainland, is far to the northeast. There are few places on the surface of the earth so far removed from other inhabited areas. This, as we shall see, has affected the history of the islands and the lives of the people.

Geologists say that the islands were formed by volcanic action. This means that many thousands of years ago volcanoes erupted on the floor of the ocean and poured out immense quantities of molten rock. As this cooled and hardened, other eruptions followed, adding new deposits of lava on top of the old. Thus, over the centuries the craters rose higher and higher. At last they emerged above the surface of the ocean and kept right on building up. Finally their crests towered thousands of feet into the air, forming the lofty mountain peaks one sees today.

This process of building up the islands still continues. Although most of the ancient craters have been quiet for centuries, there are two active volcanoes on Hawaii, the southernmost island of the group. These are called Kilauea and Mauna Loa. From time to time during the past century huge masses of lava have poured from them and run like great rivers down the mountain sides. On the way they covered many square miles of the countryside before emptying into the sea. Hawaii is thus called a "new" island, for it is still being added to by deposits of lava forced up from the depths of the earth.

There are seven important islands in the group. The largest of these is Hawaii, which is often called "the Big Island." The others, in the order of their size, are Maui, Oahu, Kauai, Molokai, Lanai, and Niihau. The total area of all the islands is a little more than 6,000 square miles. This makes them slightly larger than the state of Connecticut.

Although they lie south of the Tropic of Cancer and are therefore in the Tropic Zone, they are not, as many people believe, tropical islands. The climate and the trees and shrubs and other vegetation that grow there can best be described as semitropical.

This means that they occupy a position somewhere between the steaming hot jungles near the equator and the cooler, more temperate regions farther north. The climate is in fact one of the most even in the world. The average temperatures vary only about ten degrees from day to day and from season to season, seldom falling below 65° or rising above 75°.

There are two reasons why the island climate is cooler than that of most lands that lie within the Tropic Zone. One is the steady air currents, called trade winds. Daily they sweep in from the east and northeast, bringing with them a refreshing coolness from the sea.

Another is the ocean current. Swinging down in a great circle from the north, it makes the temperature of the water about the islands much cooler than it would otherwise be.

But, although the Hawaiian climate is properly described as mild and temperate, it must not be supposed that it never varies from day to day or from place to place. As a matter of fact, it has extremes of temperature and rainfall such as are rarely found elsewhere within so small an area. The two great mountains on the island of Hawaii rise more than 13,500 feet above the sea. These mountains, Mauna Loa and Mauna Kea, are capped with snow during parts of each year. Yet, in the lowlands only a few miles away, one finds sugar and coffee plantations and such tropical fruits as oranges, papayas, bananas, breadfruit, and pineapples.

The variation in the amount of rainfall in different parts of the same islands is equally striking. This is because the trade winds, coming in from the east and northeast, are cooled by being forced upward in order to pass over the high mountains. This causes the moisture they contain to condense into water which falls as rain on the upper slopes. Thus, the northeastern, or windward, sides of the islands receive a great deal of rain, while in the areas that lie beyond, on the leeward side, so little falls that in many places crops can be grown only by means of irrigation.

Mount Waialeale, on the island of Kauai, the northernmost of the group, has an annual rainfall that averages 460 inches. Sometimes it exceeds 600 inches, or fifty feet! This makes the mountain one of the wettest spots in the world. Yet, on the same island, less than twenty miles distant, only about twenty inches of rain fall each year. This is less than one-twentieth of what descends on Mount Waialeale.

Here, then, are some of the factors that from earliest times have played important parts in the history of the islands and in the habits and customs of the people: their position on the broad face of the Pacific Ocean; their separation by thousands of miles from other large land areas; their volcanic origin; and, finally, their mild, semitropical climate combined with the wide variation in the amount of rain that falls in different parts of the same islands.

2

The First Hawaiians

THE NATIVES WHO FIRST SETTLED ON THE HAWAI-
ian Islands had no written language. The only way
the record of past events could be preserved was
by word of mouth. For many centuries, therefore,
the stories of their great men and notable deeds
were known only through legends that had been
told and retold many times and so passed down
from one generation to the next.

From these legends and from studies of the relics

left behind by the first inhabitants, it has been possible to learn something of who the first Hawaiians were, where they came from, and what manner of lives they lived.

They were a branch of a race called the Polynesians. This is a name made up of two Greek words that mean "many islands." The Polynesians were a hearty and adventurous people. Many centuries ago they migrated from Asia and settled on the islands in a great triangular area in the middle of the Pacific Ocean. The three corners of the triangle touch New Zealand in the southwest, Easter Island to the east, and the Hawaiian group far to the north.

As navigators and explorers, the early Polynesians were more skilled and venturesome than nearly any other people of their time. Living as they did on tiny islands scattered over the vast surface of the ocean, they became such expert seamen that they thought little of traveling great distances in their native canoes. Often these voyages from

11

island to island were thousands of miles in length. In making them, the travelers had to spend many days, and sometimes even weeks, at sea.

Of course, they had no charts or compasses or other instruments to help them find their way. How, then, did they know how to reach their destinations in that vast expanse of water? The answer is that the navigators laid their courses by studying the movement of the winds and the ocean currents, by observing the position of the stars and sun, and by carefully following the flight of birds. This knowledge was preserved and memorized. It was passed on and added to by generation after generation until presently the navigators became so skilled that even the longest voyages could be undertaken in comparative safety.

There is no record of when and under what circumstances members of this far-traveling race first landed on the Hawaiian Islands. Legends repeated by the native bards and so handed down

The Polynesians brought many useful things to the Hawaiian Islands

through the centuries state that the original settlers were a people called the Menehunes.

As time passed, the Hawaiians came to think of the Menehunes as little men no more than a foot or two tall who were extremely industrious and clever. Today they would be called dwarfs or gremlins. It was said that the Menehunes could build temples, dam streams, construct breakwaters, and dig canals. They worked so rapidly that whatever task they undertook was completed in the course of a single night. (They never worked during the day.)

The Polynesians were a restless people and the first parties to come up from the south and settle on Hawaii were presently followed by others. Then, more than two centuries before the discovery of America, there was a great movement between the islands of the Central Pacific. At that time many canoe-loads of natives made the long voyage northward to the Hawaiian group.

They brought with them a great number of useful things that had not before existed on the islands. These included their three domestic animals —pigs, dogs, and chickens—and the cuttings of many valuable plants and trees. Among them were the *taro* plant—from which they made a food called *poi*—banana, coconut, and breadfruit trees, and the paper mulberry. The new arrivals were a more advanced people than the first settlers, and they took over control of the islands. Their chiefs became rulers over the inhabitants, and their priests built new temples and introduced new forms of worship.

What was the nature of these people who for the next four centuries lived in this remote spot, their very existence unknown to the rest of the world? Physically, the Hawaiian was tall and well proportioned. His skin was light brown, his hair black, and his bearing erect and proud. As for his skills, we have seen that he was an extremely able navigator and expert in the building and handling of the primitive canoes in which he made such remarkably long voyages.

In addition, he was the master of many other arts and crafts. He was skilled in the cultivation of the crops on which he depended for food, in fishing, in the building of the houses in which he lived. He was expert, too, in making the many objects used as household utensils or as personal ornaments and as weapons of war. All these he fashioned with instruments made of stone or wood or bone, for until the coming of the white man, the Hawaiian had no metals.

The ingenuity with which he overcame that handicap, and something of the everyday life of the first Hawaiians, will be told in the next chapters.

3

Life in Old Hawaii

FROM THE TIME MAN FIRST CAME TO LIVE ON
the earth, the things he most needed have been
food, clothing, and a place of shelter. This, of
course, was as true of the early Hawaiians as it was
of people who lived in other places and at other
times.

17

But because of the mild climate of their islands, the Hawaiians had less need of many of these things than those who made their homes in more northern lands. It was not necessary for them to build strong houses or to wear warm clothing as protection from the winter's cold. Living in a land where the days were always comfortably warm and the nights seldom chilly, these people needed little clothing.

The men usually wore a single garment called a *malo*. This was a strip of cloth six to eight inches wide and about eight feet long, which was passed between the legs and wrapped around the waist, with one end hanging down a few inches in front and the other tucked in behind.

The women's garment was a short skirt called a *pa'u*. This was formed from a single strip of cloth that was wrapped several times about the body, covering it from the waist to the knees. In addition both men and women had a sort of cape, called a *kihei*. This they wore for added warmth in the evenings or put on for special occasions.

The material of which these articles were made was called *tapa*. *Tapa* was made by the Hawaiian women from the inner bark of the paper mulberry tree or from that of other trees or shrubs. Its manufacture was a slow and tedious process.

First the bark was stripped from the young trees and the outside bark scraped off. The strips that remained were then soaked in water for several days to soften them. Then several strips were placed together and beaten on a stone anvil until they were firmly welded together. After another soaking in water they were again beaten, this time on the flattened log of the *kawauke* tree, until the mass had been pounded out into thin, broad strips.

Both the outside of the *kawauke* log and the beater had grooves cut into their surfaces. These formed a design or pattern in the completed *tapa*. Sometimes further decorations were added by placing red or black dyes on the stampers during the final beating, which imprinted ornaments on the cloth. Some samples of this early-day *tapa* still exist; they show that the dress of the Hawaiians was often both gay and colorful.

Because *tapa* more closely resembles paper than our modern woven cloth, it would not long shed rain, which is frequent in many parts of the islands. To overcome that handicap, the material was sometimes dipped in an oil made from *kukui* or coconuts. When *tapa* was so treated it became waterproof and so could be worn on rainy days.

The Hawaiians were an outdoor people. Usually their houses were used only as sleeping quarters and as places of shelter during wet weather. Nearly all of them were small and simply built, rectangular in shape, with low walls and peaked roofs. Their frames were made of the straight trunks of small trees, set into the ground. Other pieces were securely tied to these to form the sides and roof. Over this was tied a thick thatch, made of *pili* grass, sugar cane leaves, or other grasses. This made walls and roof that warded off the wind and shed rain even in the heaviest downpours.

The floors were dirt, over which mats were spread to serve as beds. The houses had a single low door but no windows or chimney, for the climate made heating unnecessary and the cooking was done outdoors.

Like their houses, the food of the early Hawaiians would seem very simple today, for they lacked many of the things that we now consider necessary. They had neither milk, nor bread, nor beef, nor many of the fruits and vegetables familiar in the present day. Yet, they were a healthy, active people, and there is nothing to indicate that they felt the lack of a more varied diet. For they had an abundance of wholesome foods.

The waters about the islands teemed with fish, and the men were all skilled fishermen. There was also a plentiful supply of meat from the birds of the forest and from domestic animals. Vegetables and fruit grown on the islands even in early times included sweet potatoes, bananas, breadfruit, coconuts, and certain other plants and seaweeds.

Their most widely used source of food, however, was the *taro* plant from which they made their *poi*. The Hawaiians looked on *poi* much as today we look on bread—something to be eaten at every meal. *Taro*, the source of *poi*, was usually grown in the lowlands, in small fields that were first enclosed in dikes and flooded with water, for it needed a great deal of moisture in order to thrive.

When the plant was fully grown it was pulled up and its thick root (which Mark Twain, who visited the islands in 1866, said looked much like a "corpulent sweet potato") was steamed or baked until it was soft. The outer skin was then peeled off and the root was placed in a wooden trough and beaten to a pulp with a stone pounder. During the pounding, water was added until the mass was reduced to a thick paste not unlike bread dough in appearance, although it was purple in color.

In this form the *poi* would last for many days. It was wrapped in the leaves of the *ti* plant and stored away in gourds or large wooden containers

22

until it was ready to be used. At mealtime a part of it was removed, and water was added to make a thinner paste. This was placed in a wooden bowl; and as the family sat about, each member dipped into the bowl and scooped up the *poi* with his fingers.

Poi is still a daily food for many Hawaiians and is offered for sale in stores in most parts of the islands. Newcomers sampling it for the first time seldom find its unfamiliar flavor very pleasant to the taste. On closer acquaintance, however, many grow to like it.

The early Hawaiians' method of cooking would seem very odd today. They had no metal utensils and were unfamiliar with ways of making pottery from clay or other products. This meant their food could not be cooked by placing it in pots or pans directly above the fire.

To boil food the islanders used a method somewhat like that once employed by the American Indians. That is, they heated stones over an open fire; then, when the stones had become very hot, they dropped them into a gourd or wooden vessel filled with water, causing the water to boil. From time to time new stones were added to keep the water boiling, and this was continued until the food was cooked.

This, however, was a slow and laborious process, and most of the cooking was done in a sort of underground oven which was called an *imu*. To make an *imu* a shallow hole was scooped in the ground and its bottom and sides were lined with rocks. Inside a fire was laid. It was kindled by rapidly rubbing together two pieces of wood, one very hard and the other so soft and porous that it was easily ignited.

When the fire had burned for some time, the *imu's* lining of rocks was thoroughly heated. Then the food was laid in the bottom, and the whole covered with leaves of the banana or the *ti* plant to keep the heat from escaping. The whole was then left until the food was cooked. In this way not only sweet potatoes and other vegetables were prepared, but also fish, birds, and chickens. On feast days, pigs and dogs, both of which the early Hawaiians regarded as rare delicacies, were roasted in the *imus*.

4

Arts and Crafts

LIVING AS THEY DID SO MANY HUNDRED MILES
from other lands and people, the early Hawaiians
had to produce for themselves everything they
needed to sustain life.

But they were an industrious and clever race
who made skillful use of the materials that lay
close to hand, fashioning them into a great many
articles that were both useful and ornamental.

Because nearly all their food came from the sea or from the fields where they grew their *taro* and other crops, the Hawaiians usually made their homes close to the shoreline. There the soil was more fertile than higher up on the mountain sides, and the fishing grounds were near by. The islanders had few villages and no large towns. Their houses were scattered, either singly or in small groups, in the lowland valleys or beside the beaches.

As has been said, the chief crop was the *taro* plant. Two varieties of *taro* flourished there, and different methods were used to grow each. One was called dry-land *taro*. This was planted in the uplands in little clearings in the forest that were rich in leaf mold and sheltered from the winds.

Most widely raised, however, was the so-called wet *taro*. To cultivate that was more difficult. We have learned that before the young plants could be set out the fields had to be made level and enclosed in dikes into which water was allowed to run until the whole surface was covered to a depth of several inches.

In terracing the *taro* fields and in building the ditches in which water was carried from the streams, the Hawaiians showed great skill. Moreover, it was their custom to set out young plants several times each year so that new crops could be harvested every few months. Thus, they always had a supply of ripe *taro* out of which to make *poi*.

Their other main source of food was the sea, and the Hawaiians were no less expert as fishermen than as *taro* farmers. Because they, and their ancestors for many generations, had lived close to the sea, they had learned the habits of the many kinds of fish that lived in the surrounding waters and the best method of catching each. Among the devices they used were nets of several types, lines and hooks of various sizes, together with traps, spears, lures, and many kinds of bait.

The making of these objects was a long and difficult task, for metals were unknown to them. Whatever they manufactured had to be fashioned out of such materials as were available. Fishhooks were patiently carved from tortoise shells or bones, with no other cutting tools than tiny stone adzes. The edges of these tools were sharpened by rubbing them against rough-textured rocks that served as grindstones.

Nets and lines were made from the fiber of a forest plant called *olona*. These possessed great strength and had the added advantage of not being injured by prolonged use in salt water. Some nets were small enough to be used by lone fishermen. Others were hundreds of feet in length, and scores of men were needed to operate them.

Fishing was done both in the shallow waters close to shore and in the open sea. Many of the fish that lived near the beaches were caught by the women. For deep-sea fishing, the men paddled far out in their outrigger canoes. Sometimes as many as twenty canoe-loads took part in the day's sport.

The schools of fish offshore were located in several ways. Sometimes the fishermen watched the movement of the birds. Sometimes they stationed keen-eyed lookouts on high cliffs above the sea, who watched for fish and signaled their position to the fishermen in the canoes. Both lines and nets were used on these expeditions and a number of different lures and baits, depending on the kind of fish being sought.

When the day's catch was brought ashore it was divided among the fishermen, and a feast usually followed, in which all took part. What was not eaten then by the fishermen and their families and friends was exchanged with other natives for *taro*, fruit, or other articles, for the Hawaiians were great traders. If any of the catch was left over, it was salted and dried and stored away for future use.

Many examples of the native Hawaiian handicrafts have come down to us and are preserved in museums in Honolulu and elsewhere. Visitors who see them today wonder how articles so useful, and so graceful and strong, could have been made with the primitive tools the early artisans had to work with.

Perhaps the most striking of all were the native canoes. These were of several types and many different sizes. For like all island people, the Hawaiians were as much at home on the water as on dry land. It was natural, therefore, that they should spend much time and skill building the sturdy, seaworthy craft in which long voyages from island to island could be made with speed and safety.

Building a canoe was a long and difficult task for the Hawaiians, handicapped as they were by the lack of metal tools. First of all the builders went into the forests high on the mountain sides and looked for a tall, straight *koa* tree from the trunk of which the hull could be made. Before deciding which tree to choose, they carefully watched the movements of one of the forest birds called the *elepaio*. If the *elepaio* ran quickly up and down the length of the trunk, it was a sign that the trunk was sound. But if the bird paused and pecked at the bark, the canoe-makers rejected it and looked for another tree. They knew that the *elepaio* fed on certain insects. If these were present in the tree's bark, defects were likely to be found in the wood underneath.

Having chosen their tree, the workmen set about chopping it down with the heavy stone adzes they used for axes. A section of its trunk, the length of the finished craft, was then cut off. Then slowly, carefully, the wood of the *koa* was hollowed out and the sides chipped away.

Little by little, after many days of exacting work, the log became a light and graceful canoe with sides only a few inches thick. The canoe was so cleverly shaped that when it was placed in the water it floated at just the right depth and on an even keel.

The boat builders, who were a special, highly trained class of workmen, made three kinds of canoes. One of the most common and useful of these was what is known today as an outrigger. This type had attached to its port—or left—side, a long, slender "outrigger" made from a piece of light, buoyant wood. The outrigger was usually carved from the trunk of the *wiliwili tree*. It extended six feet or more from the hull of the boat.

The advantage of the outrigger canoe, which is still to be seen in the waters about the islands, is that it is almost impossible to capsize. Thus, it can safely be launched through even heavy surfs.

Another type was the double canoe, which consisted of two hulls firmly lashed together with a platform or deck between. It was in such craft that the ancient Hawaiians made their long voyages to and from the distant islands to the south.

33

Besides building their houses and canoes and manufacturing the *tapa* with which they clothed themselves, the early workers made a great number of other useful articles. These included such household utensils as wooden platters and bowls and other food containers, brooms, lamps, mirrors and woven mats, tools for cultivating their fields, and the spears, clubs, and other weapons needed during their frequent wars.

But the old-time natives had also a love of beauty, and much time and care were spent in making objects of personal adornment either for themselves or, more often, for their chiefs. These included not only the flower *leis*, or wreaths, familiar to every visitor to the islands today, but also bracelets and necklaces made from brightly colored sea shells or from the teeth of animals or human beings.

Other highly prized ornaments were anklets consisting of many dogs' teeth loosely strung together. When these were worn by the native

Little by little the log became a light and graceful canoe

dancers, they gave off a rhythmic clicking sound as their wearers went through the steps of their dances.

The most striking of the native ornaments, however, were the splendid feather robes, capes, and helmets worn by the kings and high chiefs. In making these garments the Hawaiians displayed a degree of skill and artistic taste seldom equaled by other primitive people. Their manufacture was an exceedingly long and exacting task. The making of a single feather robe might occupy a large group of skilled workmen for many months or sometimes even years.

The first step was to prepare a finely woven net the size and shape of the completed robe. This was made from the slender fibers of the *olona* plant. On its surface many thousands of tiny feathers were then tied, one by one in even, closely spaced rows. These were so skillfully arranged that the completed garment had an appearance as smooth and colorful as the breast of a tropical bird.

Gathering the feathers for these splendid robes —which were worn on special occasions by the rulers as a mark of their authority—was in itself an exceedingly long and tedious task. This was entrusted to a specially trained group of hunters called the *poe hahai*, a native word that means feather-gatherers. The *poe hahai* made their way into the thick forests of the interior and trapped the birds from which the feathers were plucked.

In the trees where these birds often perched, the hunters placed sticks covered with a thick, gluelike paste. Birds lighting on them were held fast until the huntsmen returned. Their captors would then remove little tufts of bright yellow feathers that grew above and below the birds' tails. Then they would release the birds, for they knew that by the next season their yellow feathers would have grown out again.

The prevailing color of the feather robes and capes was yellow. However, some garments were ornamented with a design of feathers of a contrasting color, usually red or black. A few examples of these masterpieces of early Hawaiian art have come down to us and are preserved in museums throughout the world. One magnificent robe, once worn by Kamehameha the First, greatest of the Hawaiian monarchs, is now on display in the Bishop Museum in Honolulu. It has been estimated that this one garment contains the feathers of 80,000 birds.

5

Kings and Chiefs of Early Hawaii

IN OLD HAWAII EVERY MAN, WOMAN, AND CHILD
belonged to one or another of three classes. First
and most powerful was the small ruling group.
These people had complete control over the lives
of their subjects.

Most powerful of all were, of course, the kings.

In the old days there were many kings. Each ruled over an island or a part of an island which he or one of his ancestors had conquered.

The kings owned all the land in their realms. They collected taxes from their subjects in the form of food or other articles. They also called on them to till the kings' fields or to work at such tasks as building temples, digging irrigation canals, and the like. Besides, the men were obliged to serve in the kings' armies in time of war.

Next below the kings were the chieftains. These were men of high birth or warriors who had distinguished themselves in battle. The kings gave them control over parts of their realms. They, in turn, allotted plots of land to the common people on which to live and grow their crops. The chiefs held their positions at the pleasure of the kings. If one proved unsatisfactory to his monarch, the latter could, and often did, remove him from power and put another in his place.

Closely allied with the kings and chieftains were

the priests. These, too, made up a powerful group, for they not only presided over the temples and conducted the religious rites, but enforced the many taboos that played so important a part in the lives of the people.

In addition, the priests were skilled in the arts and crafts. They supervised such activities as canoe-building and navigation. They were familiar with the legends of the past, which had been handed down to them by their ancestors and which they, in turn, passed on to succeeding generations.

Below the kings, chiefs, priests, and others of the ruling class—who were called the *alïi*—were the common people. These were by far the largest part of the population. They were known as the *makaainana* which, in the Hawaiian language, means those who live on the land. But the *makaainana* included also the fishermen, hunters, boat-builders, soldiers, and those of many other occupations.

In the division of the land, the head of each

family of the *makaainana* was given the use of a plot of ground. On this he could build his house, grow his *taro* or other crops, and raise his domestic animals. In addition, he shared with his neighbors the use of a strip of land that extended from the shoreline high up into the mountains. This gave him the right to fish in the sea and to hunt or cut wood or gather other needed materials in the forests.

Finally, and lowest on the scale, was a class called the *kauwa*. They were very poor, having neither lands nor other property. They lived in the more remote parts of the islands and were seldom visited, or even spoken to, by the other natives.

Not much is known of the *kauwa* or why they came to be shunned by their fellows. One theory is that they were descended from the group of Polynesians who first settled on the islands and who were conquered by the later arrivals. Another is that they had been deprived of their rights as punishment for having broken the law or violated one of the many taboos.

The taboo system was encouraged by the ruling classes because it was one way by which they maintained their complete control over their subjects. The kings and high chiefs were held in such awe that it was forbidden—that is, taboo—for the common people to stand in their presence. Instead, they were required to fall to their knees when their king or chief passed by.

Many other taboos governed the commoner's relations with his rulers. He was forbidden, under penalty of death, to touch the king's clothing or to allow his shadow to fall on the king. He was obliged to fall on his face not only in the king's presence but when certain of his belongings were carried past.

There were numerous other prohibitions, too. Breaking these was an extremely serious offense. To step into the shadow of the king's house while wearing a *lei* or mantle was punishable by death.

Once when an early exploring ship visited the islands, a native king came on board and went down to the captain's cabin. Immediately every Hawaiian on the deck jumped into the water because it was taboo for a commoner to stand higher than his king.

But the taboos were not all concerned with the common people's relations with their rulers. They regulated almost every phase of their everyday lives. It was forbidden for men and women to eat together or to cook their food in the same oven. Certain foods were taboo to women at any time. These included pork, turtles, and some kinds of fish, as well as bananas and coconuts. Moreover, there were periods each year when heavy penalties were imposed on those who went fishing, or lighted a fire, or cultivated their fields, or did a variety of other everyday tasks.

The taboos, however, were only one phase of the religion of the Hawaiians. Living close to

44

nature, they believed that all their activities were influenced by many unseen powers whom they looked on as gods. They could win the good will of these gods by performing certain rites.

Each god had its special sphere of influence. The four most important were Kane, who was supposed to preside over the forests; Lono, the god of agriculture; Ku, god of war; and Kanaloa, who was sometimes regarded as the god of the sea and sometimes as ruler over the spirits of the dead.

Each of the major gods had separate shrines or temples, called *heiaus*, where they were worshiped. Here offerings of food, fruit, and sometimes human sacrifices, were made to win their favor and support. The ruins of several of these ancient *heiaus* are still to be found on the islands. They are large and impressive enclosures surrounded by stone walls and containing raised platforms or altars. Standing about were great

45

wooden images with carved faces bearing expressions so terrifying as to inspire fear and awe on the part of all who beheld them.

But it must not be supposed that, because of their all-powerful rulers and their taboos and vengeful gods, the life of the early Hawaiians was all grim and unhappy. On the contrary they were a gay, pleasure-loving people. They had many sports and games and other pastimes. Most of these were enjoyed the year around.

However, there was a certain period, called the *makahiki*, when all work was put aside and all the people gave themselves over to athletic tournaments, feats of strength and skill, boat-racing, surfboard-riding, and much else.

One of the favorite sports of the ruling, or *ali'i*, class was coasting down the mountain sides on sleds with runners that slid rapidly over grass-covered runways. This pastime was called *holua*. Some of the old *holua* courses may still be seen today. Their routes slant so steeply downward that one can believe that this must indeed have been "the sport of royalty."

In a land where there were no roads and, until the foreigners came, no horses or other riding animals, messages were carried from place to place by trained runners. Great tales were told of the speed and endurance of these early messengers. It is said that one, in the service of King Kamehameha the First, could take a live fish from the sea on the eastern shore of Hawaii, carry it entirely across the island—a distance of more than a hundred miles—and deposit it, still living, in the water on the west coast. Many similar feats, hardly less remarkable, are recorded in the legends of the early Hawaiians.

Young people, too, had their games. Some were much like those played today in many parts of the world. These included top-spinning, skipping rope, flying kites, dart-throwing, walking on stilts, as well as foot races, jumping contests and, of course, swimming and boating. In the last-named pastimes, every Hawaiian child became expert at an early age.

Dancing and feasting were, then as now, favorite enjoyments of the pleasure-loving natives. In early times their dance, the *hula*, was both a form of recreation and a means of dramatizing certain of their beliefs and legends. The old-time stories were chanted by priests while the dancers went through the graceful steps and gestures of the *hula*, usually to the accompaniment of drums, flutes, or other native instruments.

The feasts, called *luaus*, were held on special occasions. To prepare for a *luau*, pigs, dogs, or sometimes fish or chickens, were baked in the underground ovens and served with *poi*, sweet potatoes, and other vegetables, followed by bananas and, for drinks, the milk of the coconut. At these banquets the diners sat in a circle on the ground, helping themselves from the heaped-up dishes or bowls ranged on *ti* leaves in the center. All ate with their fingers, for knives, forks, and spoons were among the many things unknown to them.

6

Captain James Cook

FOR MANY CENTURIES AFTER THE FIRST PARTIES
of Polynesians landed there, the Hawaiian Islands
remained unknown to the outer world. If, however, one glances at a map and considers their location in relation to other settled areas, the reason
for this will become plain. For the Hawaiian
group is one of the most remote and isolated land
masses in all the world. Throughout the fifteenth,
sixteenth, and seventeenth centuries, fearless ex-

plorers were tirelessly searching out new lands. Yet this group of Pacific islands remained unsighted and unexplored. Their very existence was unsuspected.

To be sure, certain old Spanish maps drawn in the sixteenth century show a body of land in the Pacific in a position not far from where the Hawaiian group is located. Some believe this might mean that the islands were sighted by an unnamed explorer during the early part of that century. But if that was so, the secret was well kept. More than 200 years were to pass before the world at large was to learn about the islands of Hawaii.

The man who announced their discovery was an English explorer, Captain James Cook. Captain Cook spent almost his entire adult life on a series of voyages of discovery to remote parts of the world. In 1767 he set off on what was to be the first of three exploring and scientific expeditions to the South Seas. This enterprise occupied him until his death a dozen years later.

It is with the third and last of these voyages

that we are concerned. In 1776—the same year in which the American Colonies gained their independence from England—Captain Cook was put in command of the ships *Resolution* and *Discovery*. He was sent off to find what other European explorers had been searching for for well over two centuries. That was the fabled Northwest Passage. It was thought that ships could use this route to pass from the Atlantic to the Pacific oceans without making the long voyage around the southern tip of South America.

Like those before him, Captain Cook failed to find a Northwest Passage—for the very good reason that none existed. But his voyage had other results that were very important.

Much of 1777 he spent cruising about the South Seas, where he added still other islands to those he had discovered on earlier voyages. Then, near the close of that year, he headed toward the northeast to take up his search for the mythical passage across the North American continent. On December 24th his ship passed close to a low-lying coral island which, in honor of the date, he named Christmas Island. He then pushed on into the uncharted seas of the North Pacific.

A little more than three weeks later, on January 18, 1778, a sudden stir of excitement rose on board the *Resolution*, for land had again been sighted. This time the objects ahead were not small, flat islands such as the men had encountered farther south. Instead, the islands ahead were of considerable size. Rugged mountains rose up from their shores and formed great rounded volcanic cones. Some of them were many thousands of feet in height.

The moment Captain Cook caught sight of these uncharted islands, he realized that his expedition had made a major discovery. Perhaps it was, as he wrote in his journal, "the most important . . . made by Europeans throughout the extent of the Pacific Ocean."

For two days the *Resolution* and *Discovery* continued on, always in sight of land. On January 20th, they dropped anchor off the village of Waimea on Kauai, the northernmost island of the group.

But the excitement of Captain Cook and his men at the discovery of the islands was as nothing compared to the wonder and awe with which the natives greeted these strange ships. The Hawaiians had never seen anything remotely like them. At first they did not recognize them as ships at all. For the only ships they knew were their *koa*-wood canoes which were long and narrow and lay low in the water.

These great vessels bore lofty masts, with yards and booms and elaborate rigging. Their decks were so high above the water that a man standing alongside in a canoe could hardly reach up to them. The islanders, convinced that these great objects could not be ships, concluded that they must be parts of the land that had drifted out to sea. Accordingly, they gave them the name for island, which is *moku*. To this day the Hawaiian name for ship is *moku*.

To the eyes of the wondering natives, those

who manned these craft were no less remarkable than the ships themselves. When Captain Cook and a party of his men first landed at Waimea, their white skins and strange clothes convinced the inhabitants that they were not human beings but gods. They were received with every mark of honor and respect. The people fell to their knees before them, just as they did in the presence of their kings.

It was not long until word of the coming of the strangers passed from island to island. Canoes bearing the news hurried from Kauai to Oahu, some sixty miles to the southeast. From there the tidings spread to Molokai, Maui, and Hawaii.

One of the messengers was a native named Moho, and this is said to be the way he described the strangers to the chiefs of the other islands:

"The men are white; their skin is loose and folding; their heads are angular; fire and smoke issue from their mouths; they have openings in the sides of their bodies into which they thrust their hands and draw out iron, beads, nails, and other treasures, and their speech is unintelligible."

Captain Cook remained about two weeks on this, his first, visit. He named these islands the Sandwich Islands in honor of the Earl of Sandwich, who was his friend and patron in England. The captain and his company then continued on to the northeast, where for many months they searched for a passage through to the Atlantic Ocean. But the rugged Alaskan coast and the frozen Arctic seas forced them at last to turn back. At the end of November, 1778, the ships again appeared off the islands.

This time they cruised from island to island. They examined and charted their coastlines and from time to time sent parties ashore to explore the interior and to trade with the natives. At length Captain Cook set up winter quarters at Kealakekua Bay on the west coast of Hawaii.

Here as elsewhere the captain and his men were received with every honor. Natives for miles about gathered to view the strangers. There was seldom a time when their ships were not surrounded by canoes filled with curious visitors.

When parties of white men went ashore, the native priests served as their escorts and bodyguard. The people fell on their faces before them; and the island king, Kalaniopuu, presented the captain with many of his prized possessions, among them six beautifully wrought robes made of the feathers of native birds.

Meantime the holds of the ships were being filled with quantities of provisions for use on the long voyage home. All had been gathered by the Hawaiians as a further mark of their friendship.

At last the taking on of supplies was completed, and the ships set sail. However, the Hawaiians had not seen the last of their visitors. When the little vessels were only three days out from the islands, they encountered a gale so severe that one of the masts of the *Resolution* was broken. Then the expedition returned to Kealakekua Bay while repairs were made.

As events were to prove, this was unfortunate for all concerned. For, although during their first stay relations between Captain Cook's men and the natives had been friendly, serious trouble now developed. The Hawaiians at once resumed their habit of paddling out in their canoes and visiting on board the ships. Articles made of iron were highly prized by the natives, since metals of all sorts were unknown to them until the coming of this expedition. A close watch had to be kept to prevent their making off with such objects.

One day a young Hawaiian was seen to seize a blacksmith's tongs and chisel and dive overboard. On learning of this, one of the native chiefs hurried ashore, recovered the missing articles and brought them back.

But an officer of the *Resolution* felt that something must be done to discourage further thefts. He rowed to the beach and prepared to take the chief's canoe. His purpose was to hold it as a safeguard against other pilfering of the ship's gear. Naturally the chief and his men opposed this, and

*A stone hurled by a native warrior struck Captain Cook
in the head*

in the scuffle that followed stones were thrown and blows exchanged. However, no serious damage was done to either side.

For the moment it appeared that this bloodless "battle" had been forgotten and good feeling restored. But that night a more serious incident occurred. A group of Hawaiians swam out to the second of the ships, the *Discovery*, and made off with one of her small boats. They simply wanted to break it apart for the nails it contained.

When the theft of the boat was discovered, Captain Cook went ashore with a group of armed sailors. He made his way to the king's house near by. There he invited King Kalaniopuu on board the *Discovery* without revealing that he intended to hold him as a hostage until the missing boat was returned.

When the natives saw their king being led down to the water, large numbers of them gathered about. Their manner grew more hostile and threatening.

When the party reached the beach, Captain

Cook ordered his men to hold their firearms in readiness in case the Hawaiians should attack. A moment later one of the sailors, seeing that a native chief had approached quite near the captain, fired his weapon at him. As the chief fell, Captain Cook turned and directed his men to climb into the boat and push off from the beach.

At that moment a stone hurled by one of the native warriors struck the captain in the head. Seeing their leader attacked, the men who had succeeded in reaching the boat opened fire. At the same time the massed Hawaiians rushed forward.

In the struggle that followed, the confusion was so great that no one on the ships out in the bay could see exactly what was happening. Several different accounts of the tragedy were later written by members of the expedition. One states that the captain was left standing alone on the beach after all his men had been knocked down by the clubs and daggers of the natives.

Another declares that as Captain Cook turned to enter the boat he was struck by a heavy club, that he staggered for a few paces, dropping his musket, and then was stabbed in the back with a dagger. He then fell into the surf, and as he was struggling to his feet he received a blow on the head from a heavy club swung by one of the native chiefs.

The battle continued for some time longer, with those manning the small boat firing into the ranks of the natives to force them to retreat. The Hawaiians stubbornly held their ground, however. Not until two cannons on board the *Resolution* were fired into their midst did they break and flee. Both sides suffered heavy losses in the brief battle. The islanders lost four of their chiefs and twenty-five warriors. The English explorers left behind not only the body of their leader but four of his landing party.

Today a monument to Captain Cook, the discoverer of the islands, marks the spot on the shore of Kealakekua Bay where he fell.

7

The Rise of Kamehameha the Great

DURING THE WINTER OF 1778-79, CAPTAIN COOK
and his men were supplying and refitting their
ships at Kealakekua Bay. One of the group that
made them welcome was a native chief, a nephew
of Kalaniopuu, the elderly king of the island of
Hawaii. This youth—he was about twenty years
old at the time—bore the name of Kamehameha,

which means "the lonely one."

Although Kamehameha was often on the ships of the visitors, he seems to have been looked on as just another of the group of young chieftains who served the king. No particular attention was paid to him by the members of the expedition who later wrote accounts of the voyage. One of the latter, however, Lieutenant King, once singled him out because of his warlike appearance. He wrote that the young chief had "the most savage face" he had ever seen.

But if Captain Cook and his shipmates had been gifted with second sight, they would have shown much more interest in the ferocious-looking young man. For Kamehameha was then at the beginning of a career that was soon to make him master of the entire group of islands. It earned him a place in Hawaiian history as the greatest of its sons, with the title of Kamehameha the Great.

Kamehameha's rise to power began only a short time after the tragic death of Captain Cook and the departure of the expedition for home. About 1780 the old king of the island gave up his throne and his place was taken by his son, Kiwalao. At the same time, Kamehameha was elevated to a position that made him the second in power in the kingdom.

But rivalry soon developed between the young chief and his cousin, King Kiwalao. Kamehameha thereupon joined with a group of other discontented chiefs and led their forces against Kiwalao's warriors. In the battle that followed Kiwalao was killed. The island was then divided into three parts, and Kamehameha became the ruler of the northern and western portions.

Then followed a time of almost continuous wars lasting a full ten years. In this time Kamehameha became the acknowledged ruler of all the islands. It would serve no useful purpose to relate in detail the long series of bloody battles by which this was brought about. However, some incidents of the campaigns were so striking that they were often told and retold. Now they have become part of the historical lore of the islands.

One of the most widely known of these stories relates how Pele, the Hawaiians' goddess of fire, once came to Kamehameha's aid at a critical moment. This took place in the year 1790. Kamehameha had made himself master of his native Hawaii. He was leading his warriors against the ruler of the neighboring islands of Maui and Molokai. While Kamehameha was absent, one of the chiefs on Hawaii, whose name was Keoua, gathered a strong force of men. He then set out to overrun the island. Villages were burned and people were killed as Keoua pushed northward from his stronghold in Kau on the island's southern tip.

On learning of this, Kamehameha abandoned his campaign and hurried back to put down Keoua's rebellion. His forces were engaged in driving Keoua's army back toward Kau. Then there occurred an event that made a deep impression on all the islanders. The route taken by Keoua's forces followed along the edge of Kilauea, one of

Hawaii's active volcanoes. While they were passing close to the crater, a violent eruption took
place. Heavy showers of ashes rained down on
them, accompanied by clouds of stifling gases.
More than a third of their number were killed, and
the survivors fled in panic. This disaster convinced
the natives that the fire goddess was on Kamehameha's side, and his prestige and power were
much enhanced.

As time went on, Kamehameha, who was a
brave and able leader, gathered about him other
allies. Some of them proved even more useful to
him than the goddess, Pele. For Captain Cook's
visit in 1778 had made the islands known to the
outer world, and it was not long before other ships
began calling there. Among the earliest of these
were two small American vessels, the *Eleanore*
and the *Fair American*. These, owned by a Captain
Metcalfe, had been trading in otter furs on the
coasts of California and the Pacific Northwest.
They put in at the islands in the winter of 1789-90.

One night while the *Eleanore* was anchored off

Maui, one of her small boats was stolen by a group of natives. As punishment for this, Captain Metcalfe landed a party of sailors who burned the village of the natives.

A few days later he took further revenge by having his men open fire on the canoes of the Hawaiians, which were circling the ship in great numbers. It is said that more than a hundred natives were killed in this attack and that many others were wounded.

While this was going on, the smaller of the two vessels, the *Fair American*, appeared off Kawaihae on the northeast coast of Hawaii. There, in a surprise attack, the natives succeeded in boarding her and overcoming the crew. All the crew were killed except Isaac Davis, the mate.

Also on Hawaii at the time was a member of the crew of the *Eleanore*, whose name was John Young. When Captain Metcalfe presently sailed off in the *Eleanore*, the two white men were left behind.

Although Kamehameha had taken no part in the

capture of the *Fair American*, he lost no time making Davis and Young his friends and advisers. For he shrewdly foresaw that they might prove useful in his plans for completing his conquest of the islands. The two men, elevated to the rank of chiefs, set to work and soon made their presence felt on the battlefields.

First they removed several small cannons from the captured schooner and fitted them with carriages so they could be used on land. They also trained Kamehameha's warriors in the use of muskets, for by then many of the chiefs had obtained firearms from the foreign traders whose ships were beginning to appear in steadily growing numbers.

Thus, with the help of his two white chiefs, Kamehameha was able to put down the last opposition on Hawaii. He was also able to cross over to Maui and defeat the king there in battle. This was so fiercely contested that it is said a nearby stream ran red with the blood of the slain.

Flushed with victory, Kamehameha then gathered the largest army ever seen on the islands. In hundreds of war canoes, he led them on an invasion of the still unconquered islands to the north and west. Maui and Molokai fell in rapid succession, and the invading horde pushed on to Oahu. A landing was made at Waikiki, and the soldiers marched inland up the Nuuanu Valley. There Oahu's king, Kalanikupule, had drawn up his forces for a final decisive stand. In this, the last and most famous battle in Hawaiian history, Kamehameha's forces were completely victorious. Hundreds of the defenders fell before the muskets and spears and clubs of the invaders. Other hundreds were driven over the edge of the Nuuanu Pali, falling to their deaths on the rocks below.

This victory made Kamehameha master of all the islands except Kauai and Niihau, which lay some sixty miles to the northwest of Oahu.

Several years later the ruler of those islands realized that resistance would be useless so he made his peace by acknowledging Kamehameha as king. Thus Kamehameha's conquest of the islands was complete.

8

The First Hawaiian King

KING KAMEHAMEHA WAS THE FIRST TO UNITE
the islands under a single ruler. The kingdom
he founded was so strong that his successors continued to govern the islands for almost a century.
For these reasons the Hawaiians have continued to

look on Kamehameha as the greatest of their national heroes. He is often referred to as "the father of his country." And his character and deeds are as much revered as are those of George Washington by citizens of the United States.

When Mark Twain visited the islands in 1866, he was much impressed by the profound respect with which the natives held the memory of the first of their kings. Yet Kamehameha had been dead for nearly half a century. "They are proud of their old warrior," wrote Mark Twain. "They love his name; his deeds form their historical age. . . ."

Much of Kamehameha's fame rests on the fact that, unlike many conquerors, he was as wise and able a peacetime leader as he had been in time of war. First he made himself undisputed master of all the islands. At once he put in motion plans not only to make his own position secure but also to repair the damage of war.

To the first of these purposes—that is, to building up and strengthening his own power—Kamehameha applied himself with energy and wisdom. This was made easier for him because by an old Hawaiian tradition the kings owned all the land over which they ruled. Thus, they were free to parcel it out among those chiefs who were their friends and supporters.

Kamehameha put this custom to excellent use. He surrounded himself with a group of loyal lieutenants and assigned important areas, and sometimes whole islands, to trusted chiefs. These were men he could depend on to follow out his policies.

The new king made skillful use, too, of another favorable circumstance. It will be remembered that his rise to power took place during the years immediately after Captain Cook's discovery of the islands. That of course had marked the end of Hawaii's centuries-long isolation from the rest of the world. For news of the islands' discovery spread rapidly from country to country. Indeed it was not long before the ships of other seafaring nations began touching on their shores.

Within a few short years this brought about great changes in many phases of life on the islands. For with the coming of the foreign ships, there sprang up a system of barter by which the visitors traded beads, cloth, firearms, metal objects, or whatever else took the fancy of the Hawaiians, for fruit, meat, and a variety of other island products.

With Isaac Davis and John Young as his aides and military advisers, Kamehameha used their cannons and muskets to good advantage in his battles with other native rulers. But it was not only weapons that he obtained from the ships of the foreigners.

After the fighting ended, the new king was eager to draw on the same source for objects useful to his people in time of peace. So it was that

The first cattle ever seen in Hawaii were brought by George Vancouver

throughout his reign he remained on friendly terms
with visitors from the outer world. He encouraged
the exchange of goods between them and his subjects.

George Vancouver tells of such dealings in his
records. He was the second renowned British explorer to visit the islands. As a young man Vancouver had accompanied Captain Cook on his
ill-fated visit. Some fifteen years later he returned
at the head of his own expedition.

Kamehameha made the British explorer welcome, and the two became fast friends. After
many meetings Vancouver wrote in his journal
warmly praising the king's kindness and gener-
osity, as well as what he termed Kamehameha's
"open, cheerful and sensible mind."

On his part, Vancouver conferred a great favor
on the Hawaiians by introducing into the islands
many useful plants and trees that had never before
been grown there. The explorer made two visits
to Kamehameha's realm. The first was in 1792.

The following year, after sailing along the west coast of North America, Vancouver returned to Hawaii. This time he landed from his ships a number of head of cattle which he had brought from California. These were the first such animals ever seen by the Hawaiians. Thus, the arrival of Vancouver's small herd marked the beginning of an industry that has ever since been important to the islands.

By the late 1790's Kamehameha had made his hold on the islands secure. During the next twenty years he proved himself a wise and humane administrator. He neglected few opportunities to rule his kingdom justly and to improve the lot of his people.

His first task was the repair of the damage done by the years of fighting while he was rising to power. During that period so large a part of the population had been bearing arms that crops had been neglected. Great areas had been laid waste and thousands of homes destroyed.

Kamehameha took vigorous measures to put the weed-grown fields back under cultivation. He issued orders to his chiefs to plant crops, rebuild the ruined houses, and revive the peacetime crafts of the people. Moreover, he set an example to his subjects by himself tilling the soil and in other ways taking an active part in the work of reconstruction.

One of the many examples of his wisdom and foresight during that time had to do with the cattle brought from the mainland by Captain Vancouver. When these were landed, the king issued orders that none of the animals was to be slaughtered for a period of ten years. Thus he made sure that in the future his subjects would have an ample supply of meat and milk and other dairy products.

He also sought to conserve the natural resources of his kingdom. One such move was to forbid the cutting down of young sandalwood trees. The wood of these trees was in great demand by the masters of the trading ships.

These traders had found a profitable market for Hawaiian sandalwood in China. Because the wood gave a fragrant odor when it was burned, the Chinese used it at religious ceremonies, at funerals, and for other purposes. Kamehameha banned the cutting of the young trees, so that the islands' sandalwood trade would last longer.

Over the years Kamehameha's friendly relations with the foreigners resulted in the introduction of many products of lasting benefit to his people. Among these, as we have seen, were the gifts of cattle and new varieties of plants by George Vancouver. Later visitors brought still more gifts. In 1796 cuttings of the first grape vines ever grown on the islands were brought by a British warship, the *Providence*. In 1803 a trading vessel, the *Lelia Byrd*, made a valuable addition to the islands' livestock by landing the first horses.

Hawaii's soil and climate proved hospitable to many of the fruits and vegetables and trees imported from abroad. Some of these are today widely cultivated and are counted among the territory's most important crops. A striking example of this is the pineapple, which, contrary to the general belief, is not a native of the islands but was first imported more than a century ago.

Kamehameha's encouragement of trade with the foreigners and his measures to preserve peace and promote prosperity among his people had their beneficial effect. During his long reign the islands entered into a new era. They cast off their isolation and took a small but useful place among the nations of the world. Having accomplished that, the aging king returned in 1811 to his native island of Hawaii. There he lived quietly until his death on May 8, 1819. He was honored alike by his subjects and by those of other races who had learned to recognize and respect his many statesmanlike qualities.

9

The Crossroads of the Pacific

THE PACIFIC OCEAN WAS THE LAST GREAT AREA
on the earth's surface to be explored. After Fernando Magellan's ships first crossed its vast surface, the islands of the Hawaiian group remained lost in that broad expanse of waters for more than two and a half centuries.

Captain Cook's discovery of the islands, however, quickly brought in a new and eventful phase of their history. Soon a succession of other ships began calling there. For the location of these islands made them a convenient stopping place for vessels sailing to and from the Orient.

More than 200 years earlier the Manila galleons had plied between the Philippines and the west coast of Mexico. These ships and those that followed had to remain continuously at sea for many weeks because their captains knew no stopping places. During these long voyages food, water, and other supplies often ran low. The result was that the crews fell victim to scurvy or other diseases and much hardship and suffering resulted.

Then came the news that a large group of islands existed in the North Pacific, forming an ideal place to break these long cruises. This was welcome indeed to the masters and crews of the ships engaged in trade between the two continents. Fortunately the islands were discovered at a time when such trade was just beginning to grow active again after a long period during which it had been all but abandoned. The Manila galleons had of course long since ceased to run. But in their places a considerable trade had sprung up between the Orient and the North American continent.

In its earlier phases much of this was carried on by American fur traders. Their ships took on cargoes of sea-otter skins that had been caught off the Northwest American coast. These they carried to China and sold. Then they made the long return voyages bearing tea or other products of the Orient for the American market.

The masters of these ships early formed the habit of putting in at the islands on both their eastward and westward voyages. There water and fresh provisions were taken on board. The crews were given a few days on shore and, when necessary, repairs were made to the ships and their gear.

Much of the sandalwood trade mentioned earlier was carried on by these vessels. Thus began the practice of exporting island products to other countries. This has continued ever since.

The far-ranging vessels of the New England whaling fleet followed after these pioneer trading ships. Soon they began to appear in Hawaiian waters. There they usually remained for a week or longer while supplies were taken on and the ships were made ready to continue their long voyages.

Some ships were newly arrived from their home ports. These headed far to sea where many weeks were spent hunting down whales and filling the holds with casks of sperm oil. Ships that had already gathered their cargoes began the long voyage round Cape Horn to their home ports.

So far as is known the first whaling ships to visit the islands were the *Equator* from Nantucket and the *Balaena* of New Bedford. Both arrived in 1819. These, however, were only the advance guard of a mighty fleet that during the next three decades numbered in the hundreds. For throughout that period the favorite whaling grounds of the North Pacific lay in that area. One was to the south of the islands; one was in the Bering Sea; and the third was to the northwest, extending almost to the coast of Japan.

The location of the islands made them a convenient stopping place. Also they abounded in necessary supplies, and the inhabitants were friendly and hospitable. It was only natural that many whalers should stop there. In fact there were so many that the harbors were often crowded and the seaside towns and villages overrun with their seamen. It is said that at Lahaina, on the island of Maui, as many as 400 such ships called there during a single season.

It was much the same at other island ports. In the spring of 1846 Henry L. Sheldon, who had just arrived from the United States, thus described the scene at Honolulu:

"There were more than one hundred whaleships in the harbor, closely packed, three or four side by side, coopering oil, discharging into homeward bound whalers or merchant vessels, and preparing for the summer's cruise in the northern seas. . . . The port, as may be supposed, presented a busy scene. Each of the one hundred or more ships had on an average thirty persons attached to it as seamen or officers, amounting in the aggregate to some three thousand persons, about one half of whom were always on shore 'on liberty,' and they gave the town quite a lively appearance. . . ."

Not all the thousands who came each year aboard the whalers or trading vessels rejoined their ships when they left port. Some were attracted by the ease of life on the islands, the mild and pleasant climate, and the friendly natives, and chose to remain behind. To be sure, some of these presently grew tired of life ashore and shipped out again on other vessels. There were, however, many who found the islands so much to their liking that they took up permanent residence there. They formed the nucleus of what later became a large and influential foreign colony.

This group, however, was very small during the first years of Kamehameha's reign. As we have seen, two of the pioneers were John Young and Isaac Davis. They were the seamen who joined the young chief in 1790 and gave him valuable aid in his struggle to complete his conquest of the islands.

Four years later, in 1794, the number of foreigners had grown to about a dozen. All were ex-seamen representing a number of different nationalities. Most of them were English or American. Thereafter the foreign residents rapidly became more numerous. It is said that at the time of Kamehameha's death in 1819 they numbered some 200, and that a ship rarely visited the islands without leaving at least one member of her crew behind.

During the early years there were some foreign residents living on all the important islands. But it was not long before the greater number of them had gathered at the village of Honolulu on Oahu. In 1794 the excellent harbor of Honolulu had been discovered. Six years later it had become the port where much of the trade with foreign ships was carried on.

The importance of the little town on the bay shore increased in 1795 when King Kamehameha established his court near by. Honolulu thereupon became the leading city of the islands.

It was there that goods produced on the other islands were brought for sale to the Yankees or other traders. There, too, the Hawaiians purchased from the stocks of the trading ships such articles of foreign manufacture as cloth, firearms, knives, liquor, beads and other ornaments.

With Honolulu the center of the islands' foreign trade, Kamehameha, copying the ways of other rulers, imposed harbor fees on vessels using the port. This brought in so much money that the king was able to buy almost any foreign goods that took his fancy. Thus, he bought muskets and cannons for the royal arsenal, ships in which to visit other parts of his realm, elaborate uniforms for his soldiers and members of his court, furniture, carpets, silverware, and other luxuries.

On his death, a warehouse full of miscellaneous belongings was found, few of which he had ever used. For in spite of his buying sprees Kamehameha shunned personal display.

During the early years the Honolulu trade was carried on either on board the ships or in a cluster of thatched houses that sprang up on the beach. As time passed, however, this informal way of doing business was discarded. Instead, some of the foreigners set themselves up as storekeepers. They bought stocks of goods from the incoming ships and sold them the products of the islands.

Thus, by 1825, in Honolulu and to some extent in other towns, the business life of the islands was largely in the hands of the newcomers.

The coming of the foreigners had of course influenced the ways and habits of the natives to some extent. But in general they continued to live as their ancestors had for generations. They cultivated their crops of *taro* and sweet potatoes, raised pigs and chickens, practiced their native crafts of weaving mats and making *tapa* cloth. And, like their forefathers, they spent much time hunting and fishing and boating. They were quite content to allow the growing commercial life of their islands to fall into the hands of the newcomers.

10

The Reign of Liholiho

UPON THE OLD KING'S DEATH IN THE SPRING OF
1819, he was followed in office by his son, Liholiho,
then a young man in his early twenties. Liholiho
assumed the title of Kamehameha the Second. He
ruled only five years, but his short reign was a
decisive one in the history of the islands. For during that time several events took place that had a

strong influence on the course of affairs in the kingdom and brought about important changes in the life of the people.

The first major happening of Liholiho's reign occurred only a few months after he took office. This was the end of the harsh and unjust taboo system under which the Hawaiians had lived for many generations. It took a great deal of courage for the young king to bring about this reform, for it meant abandoning the ancient religion of the people. Many of his subjects, including not only the native priests but some of his most powerful chiefs, bitterly opposed the change.

The king, however, would not be turned aside from his purpose. To the day of his death the elder Kamehameha had upheld the taboo system. But Liholiho realized that the coming of the white men had ushered in a new era in the islands' history. Many of the old laws and customs which the natives had once accepted without question were becoming more difficult to enforce.

Fortunately, in this matter Liholiho had a valuable ally in the dowager queen, Kaahumanu, the widow of Kamehameha the First. When Liholiho became king, Kaahumanu was made *kuhina-nui*, or, as we would say, prime minister. This made her the second most powerful official in the kingdom. Kaahumanu was a woman of spirit and strong will, who had learned much of the ways of the foreigners. She was eager to free the island women from the taboos that had always been far more severe on them than on the men. At her urging Liholiho at length decided to act.

He chose a highly dramatic way to announce to his people that the taboo system had been abolished. As has been stated, one of the most strictly enforced taboos was that which forbade men and women to eat together or to prepare their food in the same ovens. When Liholiho had reached his decision, in November of 1819, he prepared a great court feast at Kailua on the Kona coast of the island of Hawaii. To it he invited many of the most important chiefs together with several influential foreigners.

When the guests arrived they found two long tables set, one for the men and one for the women. After the feast had begun, Liholiho suddenly got up from his place at the head of the men's table. He crossed over to where the women were eating, took a vacant place on the mat there, and continued his meal. The guests—excepting a few who had been told in advance what was going to happen —were both surprised and shocked at this action, for it violated one of the oldest of the native taboos. Many feared that it would bring down on the king the wrath of the ancient Hawaiian gods.

However, when it became clear that no harm was to come to him or his people, Liholiho announced the abolishment of the other taboos. At the same time he ordered the destruction of all the temples and images. This was deeply resented in many quarters. However, those who rose in revolt

Liholiho and his wife were given a warm reception in London

found few supporters among the common people and the disorders were quickly put down.

Even the king's orders, supported by most of the chiefs, could not at once persuade the natives to abandon entirely the customs they and their forefathers had followed for so long. Here and there throughout the islands the priests and others prevented the destruction of their idols by hiding them in caves and other remote places. There they were worshiped in secret for some years longer.

But as time passed and contacts with the outer world grew closer, further sweeping changes took place in the lives and habits of all classes. The ruling group, as we have seen, were among the first to adopt the ways of civilization.

King Liholiho was himself a leader in this movement. Unfortunately, his admiration for the customs of the white men was so keen that he copied not only their virtues but their vices too. The result was that he spent more and more time drinking and gambling. He indulged in reckless extravagances that at times threatened to bankrupt the little kingdom.

The funds flowing into the royal treasury from harbor fees and the profitable sandalwood trade were freely spent for luxuries brought to the islands on the trading ships of the foreigners. Thus, the houses of the king, of members of his court, and of the more powerful chiefs, were presently crowded with expensive goods. Many of these were useless to their owners.

At state functions the ladies of the court decked themselves out in the finest silks and jewels and embroideries, and the men in elaborate uniforms. Also, great stocks of the choicest liquors were assembled in the royal storehouses, together with heavy chests of silverware, plates and glasses, furniture, carpets, and much else. It is said that during Liholiho's reign shrewd traders sold whole shiploads of such goods to the king. This enriched the traders and all but emptied the royal treasury.

The rank and file of the people, of course, did

not share in these luxuries from beyond the seas. Yet, in many ways their lives, too, were profoundly changed by the passing of the old order. The islanders had for centuries been a seafaring people. From childhood they had been familiar with life on the water and highly skilled in the handling of their native canoes. It was not long before the masters of the foreign ships realized that the natives made excellent seamen and began signing them on as members of their crews.

Within a few years scores, and later hundreds, of natives were sailing the seven seas and seeing the distant ports of the world. Many joined the ships of the whaling fleet, where they proved especially skilled in the handling of small boats. Some rose to the responsible posts of harpooners. All this served still further to break down the old-time isolation and to make Liholiho's island kingdom known to the rest of the world.

Nearly five years after he ascended to the throne the final great event of Liholiho's reign occurred.

In the fall of 1823 he embarked on an English whaler for a visit to London. With him were his young wife, Kamamalu, and a party of advisers and attendants. In London Liholiho planned to strengthen the bonds between his small country and the great empire under whose protection he hoped to place the islands. In order to pay the expenses of the journey he took along a chest containing $25,000 in gold coins. However, during the long voyage his old weakness for gambling got the better of him, and when the ship reached England the kingly treasure chest was half empty.

But this misfortune was forgotten in the warmth of his reception at the British capital. Liholiho and his party became the guests of the empire. They were put up in elaborate quarters at London's finest hotel and at once plunged into a succession of banquets, receptions, and sightseeing trips.

But after a few weeks this round of pleasures came to a tragic end. Several members of the party, among them Queen Kamamalu, were stricken with the measles. This disease, mild enough to those races that had known it for generations, proved serious indeed to the Hawaiians. On July 8, 1824, the popular young queen died. King Kamehameha the Second had meantime caught the malady. He survived Kamamalu by only six days.

The bodies of the royal couple, accompanied by the saddened members of their party, were carried back to the islands on board the British warship, *Blonde*. Upon reaching Honolulu the royal couple were given a great state funeral by their sorrowing subjects.

11

Last Years of the Kingdom

BEFORE KING LIHOLIHO SET OFF ON HIS ILL-FATED voyage to England, he named as his successor his younger brother Kauikeaouli, who was then a lad of nine. And to rule over the kingdom during his absence Liholiho selected Kaahumanu, the dowager queen, who throughout his brief reign had been the most influential of his advisers. Thus, after Liholiho's death, Kaahumanu became the virtual ruler of the kingdom during the childhood and youth of Kauikeaouli, who became known as Kamehameha the Third.

The new king's reign lasted twenty-nine years, from 1825 to 1854. It was a period during which many stirring events took place, bringing great changes to the people of the islands. Relations with the outer world were growing closer, and the number of foreign residents was increasing steadily. Hence, old beliefs and customs had one by one to be discarded. It was no longer possible, as it had been in the old days, for the king to rule as an absolute monarch. Both the settlers from other lands and the Hawaiian people themselves were beginning to demand a government better adapted to the new conditions.

Kamehameha the Third was a wise and just ruler, and he fully sympathized with these aspirations. When he grew old enough to assume his duties as king, he actively supported efforts to liberalize the government and to better the lot of his subjects.

The most important of his many reforms was

what became known as the great *mahele*. That decree marked the end of the ancient custom that made the king sole owner of all the land in his realm. Instead it was divided into three equal parts.

One part the king retained as his personal property. One part was divided among the chiefs, and the remaining third was given to the people. Of his own share, the king then gave one-half to his subjects, and many of the chiefs followed his example.

By the *mahele*, some 12,000 heads of families were given title to pieces of land ranging in size from one-third of an acre to forty acres. For the first time, too, foreigners were allowed to own the land on which they lived or where they had their places of business.

Unfortunately, this plan for bettering the lot of the common people did not work out so well as its sponsors had hoped. For neither they nor their ancestors had ever owned any property except a few personal possessions that could be carried about from place to place. The average native was naturally of a roving disposition, ever ready to wander here and there as the fancy moved him. To settle down on a farm of his own and live there permanently was a new experience and one that failed to appeal to him. The result was that he had no qualms about selling his land for whatever might be offered. Or he might trade it for some object of trifling value, or, failing that, simply move away and abandon it.

Thus, within a few years a great deal of the most productive land on the islands passed into the possession of others. In nearly every case the new owners were foreigners who had become permanent residents. Some of the latter presently controlled vast holdings. This fact was to have an important effect on the future economy of the islands.

Many of the other happenings during the reign of Kamehameha the Third had to do with relations between his small kingdom and the other nations of the world. For, beginning only a few years after Captain Cook's discovery, there had been a growing rivalry between a number of seafaring countries to extend their influence over the islands and to control their trade. These included England, France, Russia, and, later, the United States. All during the 1830's and 1840's a series of incidents growing out of these rivalries took place. First one nation and then another sought to protect its interests or to gain an advantage.

Throughout the earlier period the influence of the British was stronger than that of any of the other powers. This was chiefly because of the wise and skillful diplomacy of Captain George Vancouver during his visits to the islands in the 1790's. The friendship that sprang up between him and Kamehameha the First laid the foundations for close ties between the two countries. These, as we have seen, were strengthened by Liholiho's journey to the British capital in 1823.

Kamehameha the Third carried on that tradition. But there was opposition from other nations whose citizens had a growing stake in the commercial life of the kingdom.

Some of these conflicting interests developed much bitterness and several times flared into violence. One of the most serious of these incidents occurred in the summer of 1839. A French warship, the *Artemise*, commanded by Captain Laplace, trained its guns on Honolulu while its captain presented a series of grievances. One demand was that Catholic missionaries be permitted to set up missions on the islands. Another was that French merchandise, "especially wines and brandies," be admitted on payment of a small import duty.

As a mark of good faith on the part of the Hawaiian government, Captain Laplace demanded that the French flag be honored with a salute of twenty-one guns and that an indemnity of $20,000 be paid his country out of the royal treasury. When he landed 200 armed men to back up his threat of immediate war, Kamehameha the Third and his advisers had no choice but to agree to all these conditions. So the *Artemise* sailed away bearing the $20,000. Some seven years later, however, better relations had been established between the two countries. Another French warship returned the coins to the Hawaiian government, still packed in their original chests with their seals unbroken.

A similar crisis arose in 1843. This time, however, it was the British who demanded redress for various supposed acts of discrimination and oppression against her subjects. The British warship, *Craysfort*, appeared off Honolulu on February 10th. The captain presented a series of claims, together with a demand for $100,000. If they were not promptly met, he threatened to seize the islands.

Faced once more by the threat of war, Kamehameha the Third hastened to yield on all points. On February 25th he formally ceded the islands to England. The Hawaiian flag was lowered and replaced by the Union Jack. For five months the country was ruled as a British possession.

Then, toward the end of July, Rear Admiral Thomas, commander of the British naval forces in the Pacific, arrived on the frigate *Dublin*. He brought instructions from his government to restore the independence of the islands. A few days later the Hawaiian emblem was again raised. In a speech celebrating their regained independence, Kamehameha the Third used this phrase, which was adopted as the motto of the kingdom: "The life of the land is preserved by righteousness."

There were many other difficult problems during the long reign of the kingdom's third monarch, but all were safely surmounted. When he died in 1854, the little country was at peace and its trade was flourishing.

Kamehameha the Third was succeeded by his adopted son, twenty-one-year-old Prince Alexander Liholiho. As Kamehameha the Fourth, he reigned for nine eventful years. During all that period both he and his advisers were much occupied with trying to overcome the problems created by two national trends that were yearly growing more pronounced. These were the steady increase in the number of foreign residents and a sharp decline in the native population.

This last was particularly alarming to the new

king. In 1778 Captain Cook had estimated the number of people at half a million. When the new king ascended the throne, the number of his people had fallen to less than 75,000. Moreover, it was still falling rapidly. This was due in large part to epidemics of measles, smallpox, and other diseases brought to the islands by the foreigners.

Much concerned at this threatened extinction of his people, Kamehameha the Fourth and other island leaders searched for a way to remedy the situation. One plan was to bring in Chinese and natives of the South Sea Islands in the hope that by intermarrying with the Hawaiians they would strengthen the native stock.

Another was to educate the people in the rules of health and to provide hospitals and medical care for the sick. Both the king and his public-spirited wife, Queen Emma, were active in planning and financing the Queen's Hospital at Honolulu. That excellent institution is still in existence. Over the years it has provided free medical aid to many thousands of patients of Hawaiian blood.

Kamehameha the Fourth died at the early age of twenty-nine. He was succeeded in 1863 by his brother Lot, the last of the Kamehameha line. His reign was a turbulent one, for, unlike the two kings before him, Kamehameha the Fifth believed in an all-powerful monarchy. Ten years earlier King Kamehameha the Third had granted his subjects a liberal constitution. Now the new king tried hard to regain some of the royal authority that had been given up. In this he was partially successful but only after a long struggle.

Another of Kamehameha the Fifth's ambitions was to secure treaties with other nations, including England, France, and the United States. These were to guarantee the independence of the kingdom. After prolonged negotiations, however, these projects ended in failure.

Unsuccessful, too, were his efforts to arrange a treaty with the United States by which the products of each country would be admitted to the other without the payment of tariffs or duties.

Kamehameha the Fifth, who was a bachelor,

died in 1872. Because there was no direct heir to the throne, an election was held to choose his successor. The choice fell to Prince Lunalilo. His democratic policies had made him a favorite with the native Hawaiians, and he had promised to restore the liberal constitution of 1852. Lunalilo, however, was in feeble health and died after reigning only a little more than a year.

Again an election was held. The two rival candidates were Queen Emma, the popular widow of Kamehameha the Fourth, and David Kalakaua. Kalakaua was an Hawaiian of noble birth, who had been an aide to Kamehameha the Fifth. Both candidates had their warm supporters. When the legislature chose Kalakaua, the supporters of Queen Emma protested so violently that rioting followed. Troops had to be landed from American and British warships in the harbor to restore order. The next day, however, Queen Emma renounced all claim to the throne and Kalakaua, the next-to-last in the line of Hawaiian monarchs, began his seventeen-year reign.

It was a period of much strife and turmoil. In the beginning Kalakaua had the powerful support of the American interests. And he showed promise of serving his people well. In 1875 he was able to negotiate the long-desired treaty with the United States. This permitted island-grown sugar to enter the United States duty free, and assured the rapid expansion of what has ever since been Hawaii's most important industry.

A few years later, Kalakaua departed on what proved to be a triumphal tour of the world. Everywhere he was greeted with the honor due a reigning monarch. On his return he occupied an impressive new royal residence, the Iolani Palace, which had been completed in his absence. This structure stands in a handsome park in the middle of Honolulu. Today it houses the executive offices of the government.

Kalakaua was instrumental, too, in having cast and set up outside the palace grounds a great bronze statue of Kamehameha the First. This shows the first and greatest of the native kings with a royal feathered robe hanging from his shoulders, and holding a tall spear that to the ancient Hawaiians signified peace.

Kalakaua's growing liking for pomp and display, however, soon got him into difficulties. His extravagant ways emptied the royal treasury. To replenish it he resorted to selling valuable privileges to foreigners, and to other abuses that brought his whole administration into disrepute. This led to the formation of a strong reform party. In 1887 it gained control and forced Kalakaua to accept a new constitution that stripped him of most of his powers.

The last years of his reign were marked by a succession of plots and counterplots. These ended only with Kalakaua's death in January, 1891, at San Francisco, where he had gone in a hope of regaining his failing health.

12

The Missionaries and Their Schools

MANY YOUNG HAWAIIANS SAILED AWAY IN THE
ships of the foreigners and so learned about lands
and peoples far from their native islands. Among
them was one whose story has often been told.
For he played a leading part in a movement that
was to bring about many changes in the lives of
his countrymen.

The youth was an orphan. His father and mother had been slain during one of the wars that swept over the islands when Kamehameha the First was rising to power. Like many other young men he joined the crew of one of the New England whalers. When the ship reached its home port, its master, Captain Brintnall, took the lad to live with him at his home in New Haven, Connecticut. His Hawaiian name was Opukahaia, but the people of New Haven renamed him Obookiah.

It was a curious incident that first brought Opukahaia (or Obookiah) to the attention of the people of that New England town. One day in 1809 a passer-by, the Reverend E. W. Dwight, chanced to see him sitting on the steps of one of the buildings on the campus of Yale College. The youth looked lonely and unhappy, and the clergyman stopped and spoke to him. In answer to the other's questions, Opukahaia replied that he was distressed because he could neither read nor write the white man's language.

Touched by this admission and by the youth's desire for learning, the preacher took Opukahaia to his home. There he called in several young friends who were students at the college and arranged for them to give lessons to the Hawaiian youth. Opukahaia proved to be an apt and eager student and under their guidance he made rapid progress. From the beginning he showed a particular interest in the Christian religion. Before many weeks had passed, he had formed an ambition to return to the islands and convert his countrymen to that faith.

At length Opukahaia's plan was brought to the attention of an organization called the American Board of Commissioners for Foreign Missions. The result was that a few years later, in 1816, a school for missionaries was founded at Cornwall, Connecticut. Opukahaia and three other Hawaiians then living in New England enrolled there. They began preparing to return to the islands as teachers and preachers.

Unfortunately, Opukahaia did not live to realize that ambition. However, soon after his death in 1818 an expedition was organized for that purpose. In the fall of the following year the Sandwich Islands Mission, numbering some twenty-five persons, set sail from Boston on the ship *Thaddeus*.

Besides the two preachers who were at its head, the group included a doctor, a farmer, a printer, and two schoolmasters. For the purpose of the expedition was not only to convert the Hawaiians to Christianity but also to teach them useful trades and to establish schools where they could learn to read and write. With these men went their wives and children. In addition, the party included several natives of the islands, who had been students at the school at Cornwall. These were to teach the others the Hawaiian language during the voyage and to act as interpreters upon their arrival.

After nearly six months on the crowded little brig, the party arrived off the island of Hawaii. At once two of the natives were sent ashore to explain the purpose of the expedition. They were also instructed to find out where the king was then living, for it was necessary to have his permission before the group could land and establish the mission. It was then that those on board the *Thaddeus* first learned of the death of Kamehameha the First, who had died almost a year earlier.

When it was learned that his successor, Liholiho, was at Kailua on the west coast of the island, the ship proceeded to that village. There for a time the fate of the enterprise hung in the balance. For Liholiho at first refused to permit the newcomers to remain permanently. It is said that the urgings of John Young, the ex-seaman who had long been a trusted adviser of the old king, helped persuade Liholiho to allow them to stay.

In this, Young was warmly supported by the women of the court. The latter, who had never before seen white women, were much interested in the wives of the missionaries and in the clothing they wore. The garment that aroused their particular admiration was a loose, full gown known to the Americans as a Mother Hubbard.

The high-ranking native women who visited the *Thaddeus* were eager to have such garments for their own use. They were much pleased when the missionary wives got out cloth and sewing materials and proceeded to make one for each of their visitors. For many years thereafter dresses of this type, which they called *holokus*, were worn by the Hawaiian women.

The members of Liholiho's court were deeply interested, too, in the five children of Daniel Chamberlain, the farmer member of the mission party. The youngest of these, two-year-old Nancy Chamberlain, completely captivated the noble ladies. They asked to be allowed to take the child ashore with them for a short visit. To this Nancy's mother at length agreed, for it would have been a serious affront to refuse such a request.

During the child's absence, those on board the brig were very anxious for her welfare. At the end of forty-eight hours, however, Nancy was returned to her mother safe and sound. The native women, in token of their gratitude, arrived laden with gifts for every member of the party. Thus, little Nancy Chamberlain played a part in winning the friendship of Liholiho and in securing his permission for the founding of the mission.

Having received the king's approval, the missionaries quickly established themselves. Some of the party remained at Kailua while the others continued on to Honolulu. Missions were established at both places. Soon a third station was founded on Kauai, the northernmost island of the group, and the work of converting and educating the natives got under way.

At first there were many difficulties. Teachers and pupils spoke different tongues, and progress was slow until that handicap could be overcome. One of the first tasks facing the missionaries was that of providing the Hawaiians with a written language. It was then necessary to teach the students the letters of the alphabet so they could learn to read. To accomplish that, the teachers translated into the native language a few simple school texts and Bible stories. These were printed on a small printing press that had been brought out on the *Thaddeus*.

So rapid was the progress, however, that within two years hundreds of students of all ages were enrolled in the schools. At first by far the greater number of pupils belonged to the ruling, or *ali'i*, class. The missionaries encouraged this because they realized that the welfare of the missions depended on the good will of the chiefs. Besides, they felt that the example the *ali'i* set by attending the schools would presently cause others to follow. This proved to be true, for as fast as native teachers could be trained and new schools opened, Hawaiians of every class presented themselves for instruction.

When word of the success of the first expedition got back to New England, new parties were organized and sent out. They were to continue the work of the pioneers and broaden the field of their operations. During the next twenty years twelve separate groups made the long voyage to the islands. These totaled about 150 persons and included not only preachers and teachers but doctors and skilled workmen of many kinds. The latter undertook to teach the natives a variety of useful crafts.

But although their schools were always crowded and their religious services well attended, the missionaries often carried on their work in the face of strong opposition. Some of the difficulties they encountered were of their own making. The great majority were intensely pious men and women who were unselfishly devoting their time to bettering the lot of their charges. But it is also true that in many ways they were narrow in their views and far too strict.

Many of the innocent pleasures of the natives they looked on as evil and tried to stamp out. The

Christianized Hawaiians were obliged to give up their traditional dances. They had to dress themselves in the white man's clothing, which was far less suitable to the semitropical climate than their own native costumes. And they had to spend all their Sundays attending church services or at prayer.

Then, too, the teaching of the missionaries and their growing influence over the people frequently brought them into conflict with other foreigners on the islands. In particular they clashed with the merchants and tavern keepers who sold intoxicating liquors to the natives, and with the masters and crews of the whalers and trading ships. Sailors coming on shore after many weeks at sea were eager for amusement and not overly careful about how they conducted themselves. The result was that drunkenness and violence were frequent in all the seaport towns.

Such behavior was naturally deplored by the missionaries, who felt that it did much to destroy their work among the natives. At every opportunity they urged the king to take steps to curb the excesses of the seamen and of those who catered to them. Especially did they advocate measures restricting the importation and sale of liquor. In this they met with some success. For King Liholiho was persuaded to issue orders limiting the hours at which the bars could remain open. He closed them entirely on Sundays. Later he went a step further and imposed heavy taxes on brandy, rum, and other intoxicants brought to the islands by the foreign traders.

These and similar restrictions were violently opposed by those against whom they were directed. The bitter quarrels that resulted kept the kingdom in turmoil for more than a decade.

13

The Republic of Hawaii

WHEN KING KALAKAUA'S LONG AND STORMY REIGN came to an end in 1891, the affairs of his little country were in a sorry state. The foreign trade in sugar and other products, on which the prosperity of the islands depended, had fallen off alarmingly. Business in many lines was at a standstill, and there was much unemployment and hardship. Moreover, the people were divided into several strong political parties. Each was striving to gain control of the government.

Thus, Kalakaua's successor, his sister, Liliuokalani, came to the throne at a time of crisis. There were powerful groups who felt that the kingdom had outlived its usefulness and should be abolished. Others favored continuing the monarchy but with the people having a larger voice in the government. Yet others took the opposite stand. They wanted to restore to their rulers many of the powers and privileges that had been taken from them.

Queen Liliuokalani was an ardent supporter of the aims of this last group. She was a woman of wide experience in public life. Throughout Kalakaua's reign she had been one of his closest advisers. Twice she had served as regent during his absences from the country.

Besides taking a leading part in many activities designed to better the lot of her race, the queen possessed considerable talent as a musician. One of her compositions was "Aloha Oe," which remains to this day one of the most widely known and admired of Hawaiian songs. These accomplishments, plus her personal charm, won her many loyal and devoted followers.

But Liliuokalani had, too, a strong will. Her effort to restore the monarchy to its old-time power soon brought her into conflict with many of her own people. It also won her the opposition of the foreigners. By then they controlled much of the business and commercial life of the islands and were yearly growing more powerful.

One of the major causes of unrest during that period came from the United States. Congress had recently passed a new tariff law which levied a tax of two cents a pound on all sugar imported from abroad. This made the operation of many of the Hawaiian sugar plantations unprofitable. Some were abandoned and others sharply reduced in the number of acres planted in sugar cane. This threw thousands out of work and brought on a depression that was keenly felt among all classes.

Because of this, as well as for other reasons, there had for some time been a desire on the part of an influential group to bring about the annexation of the islands to the United States. This was but one of a long series of such movements that dated back more than a century, with first one nation and then another striving to place the little kingdom under its flag.

As time passed, however, the United States came to have a decided advantage in this international rivalry. This was not only because geographically it was far closer to the islands than any other major power, but also because the Americans year by year had become more numerous and influential in the political and commercial affairs of the kingdom.

By the time Kalakaua's reign ended it had become evident that if the monarchy were to be abolished the country would in all likelihood soon be joined to the United States. For some time members of the Annexation Party, as their organization was called, had been meeting secretly. However, during the turbulent period after Liliuokalani came to power, they brought their campaign into the open and were joined by others opposed to the queen's policies. The combined groups were powerful enough to defeat Liliuokalani's efforts to restore the monarchy to its former strong position.

The contest for the control of the government continued for many months, with first one side and then the other gaining an advantage. Then on January 17, 1893, the struggle reached a climax. On the afternoon of that day the parties favoring annexation took forcible possession of the government offices and issued a proclamation declaring the monarchy at an end. The leaders of the movement then set up a temporary government headed by Sanford B. Dole. Then they dispatched representatives to Washington in the hope of arranging for the transfer of the islands to the United States.

In Washington a treaty of annexation was drawn up and signed by President Benjamin Harrison, who was soon to leave office. However, the Senate failed to vote on the treaty before the end of Harrison's administration. When Grover Cleveland became President in 1893, he withdrew the treaty from the Senate and sent a representative to Hawaii. This official, James H. Blount, was to investigate the circumstances under which Queen Liliuokalani had been forced from the throne.

The report sent back to Washington by this representative charged that the American minister to the islands, John L. Stevens, had wrongfully aided the annexation forces in overthrowing the monarchy. President Cleveland thereupon dispatched a new minister to Honolulu with instructions to restore Liliuokalani to power.

This mission, however, proved unsuccessful. The leaders of the Provisional Government refused to surrender their authority. Instead, they

131

called a convention. On July 3, 1894, the convention delegates drew up a new constitution creating the Republic of Hawaii, which took over control of the islands on the following day.

The republic, with Sanford B. Dole as its president, remained in power for nearly six years. But the plan to bring about annexation to the United States was by no means abandoned, and the subject was much debated both in Hawaii and at Washington.

Nothing could be accomplished during President Cleveland's administration. When, in 1897, he was succeeded by President McKinley, the question was taken up again and this time with more success.

A new treaty was signed in June of that year and six months later was submitted to the Senate. In September, 1897, it was approved by the Hawaiian authorities. But once again its ratification was opposed in the United States, and another long delay followed. It was not until the summer of 1898 that the treaty was finally approved.

The Republic of Hawaii thereupon ceased to exist, and the islands became a part of the territory of the United States.

14

"The Melting Pot"

SOON AFTER THE ANNEXATION TREATY BECAME law, President McKinley appointed a board of five members to prepare legislation for the administration of the new possession. The act, which was passed by Congress in April, 1900, was quite similar to those governing the territories on the mainland. The chief office of the territory was a governor appointed by the President. A representative to Congress was to be elected by the voters on the islands. This Hawaii delegate sat in the House of Representatives where he looked after the interests of the islanders. He had, however, no vote.

With certain minor changes this original act setting up ways and means of governing the Territory of Hawaii is still in force today.

But what changes have meantime taken place in the territory itself! When the islands were first joined to the United States a little more than half a century ago, their population stood at 110,000. In 1950 it numbered close to half a million.

At the earlier date one out of every three residents was of Hawaiian, or partly Hawaiian, blood. Today these make up only about one seventh of the population.

According to the 1950 census the largest group was the Japanese, with close to 185,000. These were followed by the Caucasians (93,000), the

Hawaiians and part-Hawaiians (88,000), Filipinos (61,000), Chinese (30,000), and many others, including some 10,000 Puerto Ricans and a slightly smaller number of Koreans.

It is this mixture of races, all living together as loyal and patriotic citizens, that today gives the territory its unique character. In tolerance and good will it might well serve as a model for all Americans everywhere. For one of our proudest traditions has grown out of the fact that the United States has long been a land to which people of many nationalities have come and where they have lived together in harmony and peace. Because for so many years members of all races were welcomed to its shores and molded into useful citizens, America has often been called a melting pot. But nowhere else in the nation has the bubbling of the pot been so continuous and lively as in Hawaii. For there the mingling of the races is far more complete and varied than in other sections of the country.

How did it happen that so many people of so many different races and backgrounds came to settle on this little group of islands far out on the broad surface of the Pacific?

To find the answer to that question one must go back many years. We have seen that the first people to settle there were the Polynesians who centuries ago came in their native canoes from distant islands in the south and southwest. We have seen, too, that following Captain Cook's historic visit in 1778 the ships of many nations began calling there, and that almost from the beginning a few members of their crews left the vessels and settled down as permanent residents.

A few years later, the ships of the New England whaling fleet and vessels engaged in the China trade began making the Hawaiian bays and inlets regular ports of call. The foreign colony, at first very small, grew steadily year by year. These newcomers were of many nationalities, chiefly American, British, and French, with a sprinkling of those from other countries. Most of them settled at Honolulu or at other seacoast towns, where they became merchants trading in the native products and in goods brought in from abroad. Thus, soon after the islands became known to the outer world, people of many nationalities took up residence there. They were attracted by the mild climate, the beauty of the setting, or the opportunities for trade.

However, the fact that Hawaii became in truth a "meeting place of the races" is due to another and quite different cause. It all began well over a hundred years ago. For it was then that certain of the foreign settlers first began experimenting with making sugar from the cane they found growing on the islands.

Sugar cane is not a native Hawaiian plant. How and when it was first introduced there is not known. It is thought, however, that cuttings were first brought in the canoes of the adventurous

Polynesians from the islands farther south. At any rate Captain Cook and his party found it growing there in 1778. Then the natives used it not to make sugar but for fences dividing their *taro* patches. They also liked to chew the sweet-tasting stalks.

Although attempts had earlier been made to produce sugar commercially, the first successful plantation and mill were established on the island of Kauai in 1835. Two years later the cane crop was harvested and run through the rude mill. The yield was only two tons of sugar, but it marked the beginning of what has ever since remained the islands' chief industry.

This pioneer plantation was soon followed by others, not only on Kauai but on Oahu, Maui, and Hawaii as well. All of them produced limited amounts of sugar in small mills, and most of their product was sold to the owners of the trading ships. The discovery of gold in California in 1848 and the rapid settling of the west coast of the United States offered a profitable new market for island sugar, and each year new fields were set out.

Soon a serious difficulty arose. Many workmen were needed to plant and cultivate and harvest the cane. Not only were the native Hawaiians too few in numbers to perform all these tasks, but it was work for which they had neither liking nor aptitude. Faced with an acute shortage of labor, the plantation owners began looking about for a new source of supply.

They turned first of all to China. Soon shiploads of Chinese were arriving from Canton and other ports. These new workers established themselves in villages on the plantations. In all, close to 50,000 industrious Chinese were so brought in. Some of them later returned to their homeland, but many settled on the islands, where their descendants form an important element of the population today.

But in general the Chinese were not content to

work year after year on the plantations. The majority remained only until out of their small wages they had saved enough to buy pieces of land and become truck farmers, or to open stores in the towns and villages. The sugar growers thereupon began importing workers from other countries. Many of these—some place their number as high as 20,000—were Portuguese from the sugar-producing islands of Madeira and the Azores.

The largest group, however, were the Japanese. Beginning in the mid-1880's, these arrived in such numbers that within twenty years they had become the largest nationality group on the islands. They have occupied that position ever since. The last considerable group to take their places in the spreading cane fields were the Filipinos. They came in large numbers during the years after the Philippine Islands were annexed to the United States in 1899.

Not all the thousands who over the years came from the far corners of the world to work in the cane fields and sugar mills remained on the islands. Some returned to their native countries while others continued on to the United States or to Canada, Mexico, or elsewhere. The great majority, however, made the islands their permanent homes. It is their descendants, together with the native Hawaiians, who today give the islands just claim to the title they proudly bear as "the melting pot of the nations."

15

Under the American Flag

MORE THAN HALF A CENTURY HAS PASSED SINCE Hawaii became a part of the United States. During that time great and far-reaching changes have taken place, affecting virtually every phase of life on the islands.

The population has grown so rapidly that today its total is more than five times greater than it was in 1900. But that is only one aspect of the peaceful revolution that has taken place. Step by step over the years the Americanization of the islands has progressed. Now the lives of present-day Hawaiians differ but little from those of their fellow citizens on the mainland. Whatever their racial backgrounds, they follow the habits and customs of the nation of which they are a part.

Their children attend American schools and play American games. Their cities and towns are modern and well kept, with substantial buildings lining the streets. Their parks and beaches and play areas would be a source of pride to any American community anywhere.

Part of this transformation is due to the fact that Hawaii's geographical position no longer cuts its people off from close contact with the rest of the world. Modern means of transportation and communication have removed its age-old isolation. From every corner of the globe, wireless constantly brings news which the island newspapers and radio stations promptly relay to all parts of the territory. Fleets of steamers regularly carry passengers and freight between Hawaiian ports and the mainland.

In addition, fast airplanes daily land and take off from the Honolulu fields. They reduce to but a few hours travel to points east and west that once consumed not days but weeks.

The economy of the islands has kept pace with the steady advances in other fields. Industries that fifty years ago were in their infancy have grown tremendously. Two of these—sugar and pineapples —must be singled out for special mention. For they give employment to many thousands of residents and are the cornerstones of the islands' trade with the rest of the world.

Something of the story of Hawaii's first sugar plantations was told in the last chapter, for it was to provide men to plant and harvest and process the cane that thousands of workers were imported from other lands.

However, to raise the crop successfully requires other things besides an abundance of laborers. Both soil and climate must be favorable if the cane fields are to flourish. Moreover, constant attention must be given to the plants from the time they are first set out until they reach maturity nearly two years later. During all that period the fields must be irrigated regularly, for sugar cane will thrive only in a moist soil. Great quantities of water are therefore needed. It is estimated that two tons of water are required to produce a single pound of sugar. To supply this, extensive systems of reservoirs and flumes and ditches have had to be constructed.

Stories of how this life-giving water was brought to the pioneer plantations form a stirring chapter in the early history of the sugar industry. One of the best known of these concerns the building of the famous Hamakua Ditch on the island of Maui. There two planters, S. T. Alexander and H. P. Baldwin, set out to bring water from the slopes of the extinct volcano, Mount Haleakala, to the fertile but dry plains that lay to the northwest.

The region over which the big ditch would have to pass was rugged in the extreme. At one point the way was barred by a deep gorge with sides so steep that one could reach the bottom only by being lowered on a rope. When workmen hesitated to make so dangerous a descent, one of the planters, despite the fact that he had but one arm, climbed over the cliff. Slowly, laboriously, he lowered himself on the rope until he had safely reached the bottom. The others, inspired by his courage, followed his example and the work continued.

When at last it was completed, the series of great pipes and tunnels and ditches extended nearly twenty miles. Each day it delivered millions of gallons of water to the parched fields. Since then many similar projects have been built: systems of flumes, ditches, and artesian wells by which vast quantities of water constantly flow into the cane fields on all the sugar-producing islands.

Today there are nearly thirty sugar plantations on the islands. All are big. The average size of their cane fields is about 7,000 acres. With but few exceptions, each plantation has its own mill. Together their output amounts to more than a million tons annually. This is about one-fourth of all the sugar produced on American soil.

The harvesting and milling of this immense crop is a highly interesting process. In recent years great machines have taken over many of the tasks that were once done by hand. Tractor-drawn plows prepare the land for planting and cultivate it during the long growing period. When the cane is ready to harvest, other ingenious machines pass through the fields, cutting off the stalks and depositing them in huge piles. These are followed by traveling cranes which lift the piles into the beds of great trucks that carry them off to the mills.

Before the cane is gathered, fires are lighted and allowed to burn through the fields. This destroys the dead leaves and other debris that accumulate during the growing season. It is said that the custom of burning the fields came about by chance. One day a fire was accidentally started on one of the plantations and burned over a considerable area before it could be put out. When, however, the burned field was examined, it was discovered that the cane stalks were undamaged. Moreover, the destruction of the dry leaves and other litter had made the task of harvesting much easier. Thereafter, it became a regular practice to burn the fields before the cane is cut.

Another important phase of Hawaii's sugar industry concerns the work done at the central Experimental Station at Honolulu. This is a research organization which the plantation owners established more than half a century ago. Its purpose was, and is, to improve the quality of the product and to find means of controlling insects and other pests injurious to the crop. Over the years the scientists there have collected specimens of cane from many parts of the world. By long experimentation they have developed varieties best suited to the soil and climate on different parts of the islands.

The most striking work done at the Experimental Station, however, consists in the continuous warfare against the harmful insects that from time to time were introduced into the islands on board the foreign ships. One of the most serious threats to the industry occurred in the early 1900's when vast numbers of a tiny insect called a leaf-hopper swarmed over the plantations. These little creatures devoured the growing cane stalks and left ruin in their wake. Scientists, searching the world for a remedy, presently located in Australia an insect that fed on the eggs of the leaf-hopper. These were introduced into the cane fields where they quickly brought the situation under control.

Only a year or two later a second destructive pest appeared. This was a small beetle that bored its way into the cane stalks, causing them to wilt and die. Again the hunt for a natural enemy of this new parasite got under way. For some time the search was fruitless. The jungles of Java and the Malay Peninsula were searched without success. At last, however, on the island of New Guinea the quest was rewarded. But now a new difficulty arose. For the New Guinea flies, which had held the cane-borer beetle in check on that island, all died when transported to Hawaii. It was not until breeding stations were established at two points along the way—in Australia and Fiji—that the delicate insects were at last safely introduced into the Hawaiian cane fields. Within a year or two they had eliminated the cane borers as a serious threat.

These are but two of a series of instances in which the scientists of the Experimental Station used nature's own method of holding destructive insects in check and so prevented serious damage to Hawaii's first industry.

The second most important crop is the pineapple, a fruit that in recent years has become perhaps the most widely known and appreciated of all the products of the islands. Its story, too, is full of interest. Like sugar cane, the pineapple is not a native of the Hawaiian group, and no one knows today when it was originally planted there. However, one of the first to experiment with growing the fruit was a Spaniard, Francisco de Paula y Marin, who settled on the island during the reign of Kamehameha the First. Others must have followed his lead, for by the 1840's pineapple was one of the delicacies offered by the natives to sailors on board the whaling and trading ships.

These first pineapples, however, were small, woody, and not over-sweet. They had an added disadvantage in that they would not keep long after being picked. Because many spoiled during the long voyages, they could not be successfully exported to other lands.

To overcome these handicaps another early settler, Captain John Kidwell, imported a new variety from the West Indies. This is the kind most widely grown on the island today. It is called the Smooth Cayenne. However, though bigger, juicier, and sweeter, this fruit had the same fault as the earlier variety—when attempts were made to ship it to the mainland many spoiled en route.

To prevent such heavy losses in transit some of the planters began, in the early 1890's, to experiment with canning the fruit. At first these efforts were not very successful. Presently, however, with the improvement of canning methods and a growing market for the product in the United States, the new industry became firmly established. Thereupon it began a rapid growth that has continued ever since. Half a century ago the annual output of the pioneer canneries was less than 2,000 cases. The yearly production now averages around 24,000,000 cases. Today eighty percent of all the pineapples consumed throughout the world come from the Hawaiian plantations.

To supply this market, immense pineapple fields have been set out in many parts of the islands. Unlike sugar cane, the plant does not need irrigation in order to thrive. It can therefore be grown on upland areas that are unsuitable to the other crop.

The pineapple plantations, too, are highly mechanized. Nearly every phase of the planting and cultivating is done by machinery. Then when the fruit is ready to be gathered, great mechanical harvesters pass through the fields. Attached to each harvester is a long boom that extends many feet out over the rows. Onto this boom the pickers deposit the ripe pineapples which are then conveyed on a moving belt to the bin of a truck. This carries them off to the cannery.

There the fruit is mechanically graded for size. Then it is fed into ingenious machines that quickly strip off the outer husk and remove the fibrous inner core, leaving only a tender cylinder of fruit. The cylinders next pass on moving belts to tables where they are trimmed, inspected, sliced, and packed in cans.

The filled cans then move on to other machines

*Eighty percent of the world's pineapples come from
Hawaiian plantations*

where syrup is added, the covers are sealed on, and the contents are sterilized by heat. Finally the labels are mechanically pasted on, and the cans are packed and sealed in cartons ready for shipment.

Pineapples have long been grown in quantity on all four of the larger islands, Hawaii, Oahu, Maui, and Kauai. It was not until recent times, however, that an important new growing area was developed. This is on the island of Lanai. Lanai, with an area of only 140 square miles, is the next-to-smallest of the major islands of the group. It lies a few miles to the west of Maui and Molokai. Until the early 1920's Lanai had few inhabitants, and herds of cattle roamed over its unproductive plains.

Then one of the leading firms of pineapple growers purchased the entire island. The new owners built a harbor and roads, developed a water supply, founded a town, and laid out vast pineapple fields that now cover many thousands of acres. The cultivation, harvesting, and transportation of the crop today give employment to the more than 3,000 persons who live on the island.

The establishment and operation of the big sugar and pineapple plantations were accompanied by the rise of another interesting phase of the commercial life of the islands. This was what has become known as the agency system. By it certain firms in Honolulu acted as sales and purchasing agents for the growers. The agents, or factors, marketed the plantations' products. They bought their supplies and equipment and, when necessary, financed their operation during bad times.

As time went on, the leading agency houses, which are referred to locally as the "Big Five," branched out into many other fields. Presently they had large holdings not only in the sugar and pineapple industries but in numerous other island enterprises as well. In recent years, however, the influence of the Big Five is much less complete than formerly, and the criticisms once levied against them are rarely heard today.

A third crop, less widely grown than sugar cane or pineapples yet important to the economy of the islands, is coffee. Coffee trees were among the many new varieties of plants introduced by pioneer settlers during the early 1800's. By 1850 there were coffee plantations, some of them of considerable size, on Oahu, Kauai, and Hawaii. In that year about a quarter of a million pounds were exported. Most of it went to the mainland, where island-grown coffee was a familiar and highly esteemed drink of the California gold miners.

A few years later, however, the owners of many of the Hawaiian coffee plantations changed to other crops. This was due to the introduction into the United States of coffee grown in South and Central America, plus the damage done by insect pests.

Today coffee-raising is carried on mainly in

the Kona region on the west coast of the "Big Island," Hawaii. There it is raised not on large plantations but in many patches of a few acres each. Such a patch can be tended by individual farmers and their families. Kona coffee, which is the islands' third most valuable crop, is now nearly all exported to the mainland. There it finds its chief use in being mixed with varieties grown elsewhere, for the island product adds a distinctive flavor to the blend.

16

Hawaii Today

ON THE MORNING OF DECEMBER 7, 1941, HAWAII
was suddenly brought to the attention of the entire world by Japan's surprise attack on Pearl Harbor and on airfields and other military posts on
the island of Oahu. Great fleets of enemy war-
planes, launched from carriers some 200 miles to

the north, shattered the peaceful Sunday morning quiet of Honolulu and its environs. In little more than an hour the bombs and torpedoes of the invaders put out of action all but a few ships of the United States Pacific Fleet. In addition, they destroyed on the ground scores of fighter planes and wrecked hangars and other installations. Casualties in dead, wounded, and missing were close to 3,500.

This assault plunged the nation into war and ushered in a new era in the history of the islands. The manner in which the people rallied from the blow won the respect of the entire nation. Within a few hours after the first bombs fell, the territory was put on a war footing. Martial law was proclaimed, and the military assumed command of nearly every phase of civilian life. Nightly blackouts were ordered. Schools and theaters were closed, and many of the school buildings were converted into hospitals or first-aid stations.

A Territorial Guard was organized, and its ranks quickly filled with volunteers. Hundreds of other citizens joined the air warden service or enlisted as police reserves and nightly patrolled the streets and beaches.

In these and other patriotic activities every part of the population played its full share. On the mainland there was some concern that residents of Japanese descent might be guilty of disloyalty and acts of violence.

Such fears were completely unfounded. For from whatever country they or their ancestors had come, the overwhelming majority proved themselves patriotic Americans. They were eager to help in their country's war effort. This was no less true of those of Japanese blood than of those from other countries. Later, after a thorough investigation, officials of the army and navy reported that not one act of sabotage had been committed by any resident of the islands, either during the attack of December 7th or later.

Throughout the early months of the war young men of Japanese ancestry were excluded from the armed forces. But once that ban was removed, thousands of native-born Japanese joined the colors. Side by side with other Americans, they served with distinction on the European battlefields.

Others rendered valuable services during the fighting in the Pacific. For in that area their knowledge of the Japanese language and customs made them highly useful as interpreters. Some of their number also undertook dangerous missions into hostile territory. There they gathered information on the location and strength of enemy troops. The full extent of the Japanese-Americans' contribution to the war effort is shown by the number of casualties suffered by soldiers from the islands. The records show that eighty-eight percent of the wounded and eighty percent of those killed were of Japanese ancestry.

The war years brought far-reaching changes to all the islands. They became an advance base through which passed vast quantities of men and materials on the way to the fighting fronts farther west. With every facility diverted to wartime ends, much of Oahu and large areas of the other islands took on the appearance of armed camps. Great numbers of soldiers passed through Honolulu. At one time their total was more than 30,000 a month. Many units both of the army and navy received their final training there. In addition numerous hospitals and rest camps were established for men brought back from the fighting zones.

Since the islands first became a part of the United States, their military value in time of war has been recognized. From the beginning, therefore, steps were taken to convert the new possession into an advance base. It should be strong enough to ward off any attack coming from the west and so protect the mainland's west coast from invasion.

Thus, in the early years of the century, permanent army posts were established and the develop-

ment of the great naval station at Pearl Harbor
was begun. These activities have continued ever
since. During World War II the military installations were enormously expanded and strengthened.

Hence over the years the army and navy have
played important parts in the development of the
territory. Moreover, the many thousands of serv-
icemen who have been stationed there have done
much to make the islands better known to the rest
of the nation.

The mild climate and picturesque scenery, together with the traditional hospitality of its people, have long made Hawaii a favorite stopping
place for visitors from other lands. The islands'
rise as a tourist center, however, has been far more
rapid in recent years than at any earlier period.
This is due in part to the fact that knowledge of
the area's attractions has steadily increased among
the people of the mainland.

But other factors, too, have been important. One

is the vast improvement in transportation facilities. Travel has been speeded up until sea voyages that once consumed weeks are now made in fast ocean steamers in five days or less. On the swift modern airliners, the length of the journey is counted not in days but in hours.

Another reason for Hawaii's steadily increasing popularity as a vacation land has been the rapid growth of facilities for the accommodation and entertainment of the visitors after they reach the islands. These include not only the group of resort hotels that line the celebrated Waikiki Beach at Honolulu but also a variety of picturesque inns scattered throughout the other islands. These, together with a network of inter-island airlines, plus numerous organized tours over excellent roads, make the territory's many points of scenic and historical interest easily accessible to visitors. And visitors have been coming in steadily increasing numbers. Today the tourist business is one of Hawaii's major industries and one that continues to grow in importance with each passing year.

More than half a century ago, Hawaii was annexed to the United States and became a territory. At that time the great majority of its people hoped and believed that in due time its territorial status would be discarded and it would be welcomed into the Union as a full-fledged state. The result was that, beginning as early as 1903, each of the territorial legislatures passed and forwarded to Congress petitions asking for statehood. However, no action was taken on these. The next step was the introduction, sixteen years later, of the first of many bills to make Hawaii a state.

These, too, had little practical effect, and it was not until the mid-1930's that real progress began to be made. Then, in 1935, a subcommittee of the House of Representatives visited the islands and held hearings on the question. As a result of this, a delegation of both senators and representatives arrived in 1937 and conducted a thorough investigation. This committee reported favorably on the territory's qualifications for statehood. However, it suggested that before final action was taken, the islanders be given an opportunity to say whether or not they favored statehood. Accordingly, at an election held in 1940, the ballot contained the question: "Do you favor statehood for Hawaii?" When the votes were counted, it was found that the "Yes" votes exceeded the "No's" by more than two to one.

The country's entry into the war in 1941 prevented further action being taken at that time. It was not until four years later that the long struggle was renewed. By then, however, its sponsors pushed the measure with renewed confidence, for throughout the war the loyalty and patriotism of the island people had been many times demonstrated. It was with high hopes, therefore, that late in 1945 a statehood bill was again introduced in

Congress, and another investigating committee—the third—was welcomed to the islands. Again the committee's report was favorable. Its chairman stated that the Hawaiian people were both ready and eager to assume the responsibilities of statehood.

For a time it appeared that the long battle had been won. On June 30, 1947, the bill was passed by the House of Representatives and sent to the Senate. Early the next year a Senate subcommittee, having conducted yet another hearing, reported that the islanders were "able and ready" for statehood. However, some members of the main committee felt that the bill should not be acted on until all its members had had an opportunity to visit the islands and make a personal investigation. The result was that the bill never reached the floor of the Senate for a vote.

Undiscouraged, the bill's sponsors introduced it again in 1950. Once more it was passed by the

House, and this time it received the approval of the Senate committee.

When it came up for consideration by the Senate, however, a bloc of senators staged a filibuster and prevented its being brought to a vote. But this seemed only to spur on those fighting for statehood for Hawaii.

When the 84th Congress met in January, 1954, the bill for statehood was presented once more. And once more hopes were high that it would be passed by both the House and the Senate.

All the while the people of the islands have continued to believe that someday their hopes will be fulfilled and a new star—the forty-ninth—will be added to the Stars and Stripes.

About the Hawaiian Words in This Book

Whenever we read of people who use some language different from our own, we face new and strange words. Often the names of the people are different from the names we are accustomed to. Often the cities and mountains have strange names. As we read these new words, we often wonder how they would sound if we could hear them pronounced correctly.

In *Hawaii: Gem of the Pacific* there are many such words and phrases. So that you will know how they are pronounced by the people of Hawaii, the Hawaiian words and phrases used in this book are listed on the following pages with a pronunciation guide for each.

Hawaiian Words and Phrases
That Appear in the Book

WORD	PRONUNCIATION	MEANING
ali'i	ah-LEE-ee	the ruling class in early days
aloha	ah-LO-hah	greeting
aloha oe	ah-LO-hah OH-eh	very cordial greeting
elepaio	EH-leh-PIE-oh	a forest bird
Haleakala	HAH-lee-ah-kah-LAH	dormant volcano on Maui
Hamakua	hah-mah-KOO-ah	region of Hawaii
Hawaii	hah-WAI-ee	one island of the group
Hawaiian	hah-WAI-yuhn	a native of the islands
heiaus	HAY-OWS	places of worship
holokus	ho-low-KOOS	a loose full dress
holua	ho-LOO-ah	sled or sledding
Honolulu	HO-no-LOO-loo	capital city of the islands
hula	HOO-lah	a Hawaiian dance
imu	EE-moo	an underground oven

173

Iolani	ee-oh-LAH-nee	former royal palace in Honolulu
Kaahumanu	kah-ah-hoo-MAH-noo	wife of Kamehameha I
Kailua	kai-LOO-ah	town on the coast of Hawaii
Kalakaua	kah-lah-KAU-ah	king who followed Lunalilo
Kalanikupule	kah-LAH-nee-koo-POO-leh	one-time king of Oahu
Kalaniopuu	kah-LAH-nee-oh-POO-oo	an early king
Kamamalu	kah-mah-MAH-loo	wife of Liholiho (Kamehameha II)
Kamehameha	kah-MAY-hah-MAY-hah	name of a line of kings
Kanaloa	KAN-nah-LO-ah	native god of the seas
Kane	KAH-nay	native god of the forests
Kau	kah-oo	stronghold of an early chieftain
Kauai	kah-WAH-ih	northernmost island of the group
Kauikeaouli	kau-I-kay-ah-OH-lee	king who became Kamehameha III
kauwa	KAH-oo-WAH	the lowest class in early days
Kawaihae	kah-wai-HAI	bay on the island of Hawaii
kawauke	KAH-WAH-oo-ke	a kind of tree
Kealakekua	kay-AH-lah-kay-KOO-ah	bay on island of Hawaii
Keoua	kay-oo-wah	an early chief
kihei	KEE-hay-ee	a short cape
Kilauea	kee-lau-WAY-ah	volcano on Hawaii
Kiwalao	kee-wah-LAH-oh	a young chief
koa	KO-ah	a kind of tree
Kona	KO-nah	region on island of Hawaii
Ku	koo	native god of war
kuhina nui	koo-HEE-nah NEW-ih	adviser to the king
kukui	KOO-koo-ih	coconuts
Lahaina	lah-HAI-nah	ancient capital at west Maui
Lanai	lah-NAH-ee	sixth largest of the islands
lei	lay	wreath
Liholiho	LEE-ho-LEE-ho	King Kamehameha II
Liliuokalani	LIH-lih-oo-oh-kah-LAH-nee	queen who ruled after Kalakaua
Lono	LO-no	native god of agriculture
luau	LOO-au	feast
Lunalilo	loo-nah-LIL-lo	king who followed Kamehameha V

Glossary

WORD	PRONUNCIATION	MEANING
mahele	mah-HEH-leh	division of land
makahiki	MAH-kah-HEE-kee	time of celebration
makaainana	MAH-kah-AI-nah-nah	the common people
malo	MA-lo	a loincloth
Maui	MAU-ee	second largest of the islands
Mauna Kea	MAU-nah KEH-ah	mountain of Hawaii
Mauna Loa	MAU-nah LO-ah	volcano of Hawaii
Menehunes	MEN-neh-HOO-neys	legendary dwarfs of the islands
Moho	MO-ho	native of the islands
moku	MO-koo	a ship
Molokai	MOH-loh-KAH-ee	an island of the group
Niihau	nee-ee-HAU	seventh largest of the islands
Nuuanu	NOO-OO-AH-noo	valley on Oahu
Nuuanu Pali	NOO-OO-AH-noo PAH-lee	Nuuanu cliff
Oahu	O-AH-hoo	second largest island in the group
Obookiah	oh-BO-oh-KEE-ah	name for Opukahaia
olona	oh-LO-nah	a forest plant
Opukahaia	oh-POO-kah-HAI-ah	a Hawaiian youth
pali	PAH-lee	a cliff or crag
pa'u	pah-oo	short skirt
Pele	PAY-lay	goddess of volcanoes
pili	PEE-lee	a kind of grass
Pili	PEE-lee	a chief
poe hahai	POH-eh hah-HAH-ee	plant gatherers
poi	poy	food made from the taro plant
tapa	TAH-pah	a kind of cloth
taro	TAH-roh	a vegetable
ti	tee	a plant
Waialeale	wai-AH-lee-AH-lee	mountain on island of Kauai
Waikiki	wai-kee-KEE	beach on Oahu
Waimea	wai-MAY-ah	village on island of Kauai

Index